Eve in Exile

Eve in Exile

AND THE RESTORATION
of FEMININITY

Rebekah Merkle

canonpress
Moscow, Idaho

Published by Canon Press
P.O. Box 8729, Moscow ID 83843
800.488.2034 | www.canonpress.com

Cover design by James Engerbretson.
Cover detail art by Forrest Dickison.
Interior design by Valerie Anne Bost and James Engerbretson.

Printed in the United States of America.

Unless otherwise indicated, Scripture quotations are from the King James Version of the Bible. Italics in Bible quotations are added by the author for emphasis.

Library of Congress Cataloging-in-Publication Data
Names: Merkle, Rebekah, author.
Title: Eve in exile : and the restoration of femininity / Rebekah Merkle.
Description: Moscow : Canon Press, 2016. | Includes bibliographical references and index.
Identifiers: LCCN 2016032376 | ISBN 9781944503529 (pbk. : alk. paper)
Subjects: LCSH: Women--Religious aspects--Christianity. | Femininity--Religious aspects--Christianity.
Classification: LCC BT704 .M545 2016 | DDC 233.082--dc23
LC record available at https://lccn.loc.gov/2016032376

16 17 18 19 20 21 22 23   10 9 8 7 6 5 4 3 2 1

CONTENTS

To Ben, who makes it easy

INTRODUCTION

THE FREEDOM OF LIMITS

You and I have been born into a world that's at war with boundaries. People are kicking over fences and knocking over barricades as far as the eye can see. Sometimes they're knocking over pretend boundaries and sometimes they're just pretending to knock over the permanent, immovable ones, but the one thing that is certain is that our generation here, in this moment, doesn't want to recognize any lines at all. We are a nation that has declared war on virtually all creational distinctives, but one area where the battle is especially hot right now is over the subject of gender. What began several centuries ago as a resentment of "gender stereotypes" has gradually but inexorably escalated to the point where our nation is now offended by the insulting restrictions offered to us by the very fact of gender itself. The Christians, meanwhile, have for two hundred years played their role as the proverbial frog in the pot, and, as I write this, the pot has very nearly reached boiling point—and we're not really sure how to get out of it now.

In the last twelve months, Bruce Jenner has started calling himself a woman publicly . . . and no one is allowed to argue. Even Siri will correct me if I ask about Bruce Jenner; replies will now only be offered about "Caitlyn" Jenner—and *Glamour* magazine has named him woman of the year. Incidentally, how hilariously insulting is that to all women everywhere? *Glamour* has declared that a middle-aged white man who has been pretending to be a woman for a grand total of one year is already doing it better than all the rest of us.

Of course, the science of the situation is completely set aside in these cases. Let's just run a little thought experiment. Let's say an archaeologist a thousand years down the road finds Bruce's skeleton. Will he conclude that these are the bones of a man or a woman? If they test his DNA, will they find that he is a man or a woman? The answer is patently obvious. God made him a man, and a man he still is—the only thing he's managed to accomplish is that he has badly decoupaged himself. But of course no one is allowed to say that. Admit it—you're furtively looking over your shoulder right now to see if you're in trouble for even *reading* what I just said. We're all supposed to go along quietly and pretend that Bruce *actually* managed to change himself from a man to a woman when, of course, he did nothing of the kind.

In my own state capital, all the school districts have determined that any boy who feels like a girl may use the girls' locker rooms. Nationally, people are yelling for the boycott of *entire states* because of the shockingly insensitive "men" and "women" signs on the doors of the restrooms. The Supreme Court has solemnly climbed up onto its soapbox and announced with a very serious face that marriage no longer has anything to do with gender. Boundaries everywhere are under a full scale assault. People don't want to be bound by their race, by their gender, by anything at all really. They want to be free to soar, untrammeled, through a category-less and restriction-less universe.

But this obliterating of lines is not actually leading us into a light-filled, utopian future—we're actually in the middle of watching our culture trip over its own shoelaces and fall unglamorously down the stairs. Chesterton said it best, "Art is limitation; the essence of every picture is the frame. If you draw a giraffe, you must draw him with a long neck. If in your bold creative way you hold yourself free to draw a giraffe with a short neck, you will really find that you are not free to draw a giraffe."[1] Chesterton is illustrating a very profound truth about the universe, and one that we would do well to thoroughly understand. It *sounds* as if it would be ever so fabulous and freeing to remove boundaries and restrictions, especially if you preface those words with all the right adjectives like "outdated" or

---

1. G.K. Chesterton, *Orthodoxy* (Chicago: Moody, 2009), p. 64.

"oppressive." However, we all still intuitively understand that when we step out of our pretend world of what sounds nice and into the world of reality, life doesn't actually work that way. As a for-instance, imagine a shorter than average, aspiring junior high basketball player who feels that the height advantage enjoyed by other, taller players is unfair. We feel sorry for him—he's awfully short after all—so we decide to help him out. We can't do anything about his height, unfortunately, but one thing we definitely *could* do is remove the basketball hoops. Removing the hoops would ensure that height didn't matter and no one had any unfair advantage over anyone else at all—we have leveled the playing field and made everything truly fair. On the other hand, however kind our intentions were, the only thing we have actually accomplished is that we have destroyed even the *possibility* of playing basketball. We haven't created additional basketball freedom for anyone, not even the short guy. True freedom lies in the opportunity to pursue excellence, and that opportunity is dependent on the boundaries that define and restrict the entire field of endeavor. Basketball without any hoops or lines on the court isn't basketball. True freedom *has* to recognize boundaries.

But which ones? We're Christian women, and we want to live in the way God told us to. We want to be obedient—but we're looking out over this current playing field and wondering where on earth we're supposed to stand. Old customs have been knocked sprawling; cultural norms have been overturned. Our daughters are born into the ruins of what used to be a Christian nation, and we are raising them in the wreckage of the West. What does obedience look like in this madhouse? Some women have resorted to simply looking at the past—finding some era they identify with and trying to re-create *now* what they imagine femininity looked like *then*. So they pick the era that most appeals to them, and they go with it. Maybe it's a Jane Austeny life. Maybe a *Little House on the Prairie* life. Maybe a 1950s suburbia life. Other women have just wandered out into the craziness of the present and tried to hang on to their Christianity while still embracing all the changes in women's roles that have happened over the last century in America.

Virtually every cultural boundary surrounding femininity has been knocked down—both the good and the bad. Those lines desperately need to be redrawn . . . because, as Chesterton pointed out, boundaries are essential to freedom. In the same way that the out-of-bounds lines and the fixed and unchanging ten-foot hoops in basketball are what create the court itself, and therefore the ability to play the game, so too the boundaries of gender are what create the possibility of excelling as a woman. The lines define and create the space in which excellence can thrive. But if there are no lines, if Bruce Jenner can win the game that is "being a woman," I may as well chuck it and decide to be a penguin instead.

The cultural chaos in which we are currently living has caused many to despair, and others to simply shrug and accept the postmodern crazy. But I want to argue that we are in the *perfect* moment to rethink this whole subject. Because our culture has kicked everything over, since nothing is left but rubble, we actually have the remarkable privilege of being able to think through each line before redrawing it. We can check each boundary against the Scriptures before setting it back in its place. What a blessing! What a huge opportunity! I might not have advocated that our culture burn the house down, but there is no denying that now that the demo has actually happened, it might be nice to start with a blank slate. Rebuilding the house, but this time with better closet space and less ugly linoleum, is actually a great opportunity. We are not living in the eighteenth century, bound by restrictive cultural norms which may or may not be scriptural. We are not stuck trying to tear down unbiblical cultural taboos which hindered many godly women in earlier centuries. We are not, for instance, in the position of being told that our feminine intellects are too fragile to handle the rigors of an education. We are not bumping up against a widespread notion that only the men are capable of critical thought or the ability to do difficult, meaningful work. Our cultural fight over femininity will actually be in the opposite direction—because we most certainly will be bumping up against our own cultural norms. Our fight is going to be with a culture that is antagonistic to the idea of trying to draw *any* lines of at all.

We have a fantastic opportunity in front of us, but we also have a hostile audience. We are in the position of Nehemiah—returning from exile and trying to rebuild the walls of Jerusalem while the culture outside jeers. But if I could stand in any moment, this is the one I would pick. We have a huge opportunity in front of us, and I hope we can make the most of it. The way of return is open to us—but it will require strong women who are willing to show actual courage if we truly want to bring Eve back from exile.

SECTION ONE

TWO DISTRACTIONS

As we tackle the subject of what biblical femininity looks like, it's important to first identify places where we could conceivably go off the rails. There's no doubt that starting from scratch on this subject is actually a ridiculously huge project, which brings its own attendant potential pitfalls with it. As soon as you bring up the subject of femininity and our desperate need to recover some of it, everyone immediately has their own ideas of how that should look. Or how it should *not* look. And some of those things are valid and legitimate and based on solid arguments and others of them are really not that at all . . . So let's begin by first attempting to eliminate two ways of thinking about the whole subject that are problematic and will actually hinder rather than help in this undertaking.

PRETENDYVILLE

One of the easiest and most obvious ditches to fall into is that of building our expectations on our idealized notions of the past. Many women are disgusted by what they see around them in our culture, and they wish that they lived in an earlier time where gender roles were clearly defined and femininity wasn't despised in the way it is today. They see the earlier societal respect for gender differences as much more creational and biblical, and they feel that if we could only recapture some of what our culture apparently *used* to possess, then we'd be back on the right path again. They look around them and see the charred remains of a spent fire, and they think if we could only blow some of those embers back into flame, then we could be comfortable again.

There are a number of troubles with this approach, however. The first is the unfortunate truth that it tends to be our imaginations which are captured by some other era, not our intellects, but while we're in the midst of it we confuse the two. Generally speaking, and as unflattering as this may be, when women yearn for some other cultural moment, their knowledge of that era comes from fiction in some form—either films or historical novels. When they lose themselves in a story, they can almost believe that they too live in a world where women were expected to behave like women, where the outfits were ever-so-much better than they are now, and where a wide gulf separated expectations for the men and expectations for the women. We all know the flat feeling that comes after you finish a really great book or a really good film series. If you haven't experienced it lately, you must remember that sensation from when you were a kid. It's like coming back down to earth with a bump, like having someone wake you up with a cold washcloth. Real life just seems insipid. Doubly so if your life actually *is* insipid. If a woman is living a duddy and prosaic life, fiction becomes a form of escapism, and unsurprisingly, she wishes her life were more like the lives of her favorite heroines. This can get all tangled up with her belief that our culture has lost something important and biblical, and all the categories in her head can get blurred and muddied. The argument goes something like this:

The Bible has expectations for gender roles

Our culture doesn't

Earlier cultures did have expectations for gender roles, as

witness all the books in my Goodreads account
Therefore, those earlier cultures were biblical

As a logical argument this is flawed on a number of levels, but again, it is the imagination and not the intellect that is driving this particular train. These women tend to snatch at vestiges of some earlier era and try wistfully to recreate something of that culture within the walls of their own home or on the boards of their Pinterest account. This is not only understandable, it can also (sometimes) be sweet and endearing. But whether it's cute or whether it's dorky, ultimately it's a dangerous distraction from our calling as women.

This particular approach can take many different forms. It could show itself in organizing balls where the girls wear gloves and homemade dresses inspired by *Pride and Prejudice*. It could take the form of grocery shopping while wearing seamed stockings and hair in victory rolls. It might involve moving out into the country and learning to milk cows. It could become an obsession with colonial penmanship or an attempt to bring "thee" and "thou" back into vogue. In fact, it could be a collage of all of the above. None of these things, by the way, am I making up. I have met teenage sisters who wore ankle-length skirts only, who grew their hair out to their waists, and who brushed each other's hair one hundred times every night before bed— their personal, home-brewed version of *Little House on the Prairie*. I've bumped into the thee-and-thou girls. I've spoken with the victory-roll-wearing housewives, and I've met the Jane Austen theme ball organizers.

There are a few things that are noticeable about this phenomenon. The first obvious take-away is that there is a widespread yearning among conservative Christians for a cultural expression of femininity. This is a common enough feature of conservative circles that we can at least say that much.

The second obvious thing is that very often, the decision about which culture is worth recapturing is based entirely on the outfits and surrounding aesthetics. I know that seems embarrassing, but I'm afraid it's just the plain truth. Some women love the Scarlett O'Hara dresses, and they like the pillars on the plantation houses, and the accent is adorable, and mint juleps just look so fun. Others are drawn toward the plucky pioneer look, the windswept prairie, and living off the land. Still more have their imaginations captured by the complicated etiquette of Regency England and the stunning landscape of the Cotswolds. The decision about which culture to emulate ends up not being based on definite knowledge of which culture was the most biblical—it really comes down to what houses and dresses are the most appealing. The sad conclusion, in the end, is that this entire phenomenon is escapist rather than principled, and is driven by wishful thinking rather than hard-headed conviction.

The whole approach is just terribly problematic. It's retreatist, it's unprincipled, it's ineffective, and it's ignorant.

Why ignorant? Honestly, the women who wish they could recapture a particular moment from history usually know very little about the *actual* history. Their knowledge is most often based on fiction. *Fiction.* A miniseries or a set of novels does not an accurate historical picture make. A little bit of research into Regency England would show us that, despite the fact that the dresses may have been cute, the society was actually horrifically corrupt. Yes, the BBC *Pride and Prejudice* series just seems so wholesome and proper and upstanding that it may be hard to believe, but if you just take a moment to research the life of Lord Byron, a flagrantly immoral, bisexual, incestuous, and nonetheless greatly admired celebrity during Jane Austen's life, or the goings-ons of the Prince Regent and his compadres during the time that she was writing her books, you would very soon discover that the Kardashians have nothing on these people. An attempt to recreate that society, especially based on the cockeyed notion that it was a *godly* society, would be utterly nonsensical.

And, truth be told, I think that often the women who fall into this particular hobby actually know that they aren't *really* going to transform our culture this way. I think they know that it's escapist. It's just more comfortable to create a pretend world, cozily tucked away from the scariness of the real world—the one that contains an awful lot of sin and ugliness. Sometimes there's fear mixed in there as well; a belief that perhaps we could shield our children or our husbands from the temptations and atrocities of our society by attempting to create a home in some distant imaginary place where everyone behaves themselves and speaks politely and drinks tea.

But God hasn't called us to run away from the world. On the contrary, in 1 Corinthians 5:10 Paul explicitly says that he doesn't expect us to live our lives without ever coming into contact with the paganism that surrounds us. "I wrote to you in my epistle not to keep company with sexually immoral people. Yet I certainly did not mean with the sexually immoral people of this world, or with the covetous, or extortioners, or idolaters, since then you would need to go out of the world." Paul expects the Christians to live in such a way that there is a marked difference between their lifestyle and that of the surrounding unbelievers, but he certainly assumes that they would be in living distinctively *in the midst of* surrounding ungodliness. He doesn't want us to run away from the world; he actually expects us to charge *at* the world. To *change* the world. The last instructions that Christ gave to his church before he ascended into heaven were to go and "baptize the nations." Those are our marching orders. We're not supposed to baptize a few people from every nation, we're supposed to baptize *the nations.* That involves winning entire *cultures* over to Christ, not just a few individual hearts.

Christ expects his church to launch a full scale assault on the world. Think of Christ's promise to Peter in Matthew 16:18. "And I tell you, you are Peter, and on this rock I will build my church, and the gates of Hell shall not prevail against it." If you think about that for a second, there's something very key that sometimes escapes people's notice. What are gates for? Are they offensive weapons or defensive? If Christ is promising that the gates of Hell shall not prevail against the church, what does that imply about the actions and position of the church? Right. The church is the army that is charging, not the one that's on the run. We are supposed to be besieging the strongholds—and that command was given to the church, the body of Christ, which includes both the men and the women. This command is most emphatically not just to the men.

The Great Commission is the New Covenant expansion of the Creation Mandate given to the human race in Genesis. Initially our job was to fill the earth and subdue it (Gen. 1:28). Now there's an additional component: we need to convert and baptize the world (Matt. 28:19). Throw your mind back to Genesis. What critical ingredient was Adam missing when he was first created? He needed a helper. By himself, Adam was incapable of doing his job, incapable of either filling the earth or subduing it. So God created a helper suitable for the job. Woman was not an afterthought, or just someone for Adam to talk to, or someone who would make him sandwiches while he did all the filling and subduing of the earth. She was essential to the entire program. When God gave Eve to Adam, He was handing Adam an amplifier. Adam alone is just Adam. Adam with Eve . . . becomes the human race. Adam is the single acorn sitting on the driveway which, no matter how hard he tries, remains an acorn. Eve is the fertile soil which takes all the potential that resides in that acorn and turns it into a tree, which produces millions more acorns and millions more trees. Eve *is* fruitfulness.

And if the Great Commission is the expansion of the Creation Mandate, if it is an unpacking of God's command in Genesis, then surely we see that women are integral to this project as well? The job of taking the world for Christ cannot be done by the men while we women sit off to the side and amuse ourselves with tea parties and having the occasional baby. If we take ourselves out of the game, the men cannot possibly accomplish what they are supposed to accomplish any more than Adam could have filled the earth on his own. We are integral to this project, and it's absolutely critical to the gospel mission that we recover a sense of our role.

2.

THE MYTHICAL FOUNTAIN
OF FULFILLMENT

The ancient Greeks told a story of Atalanta, a beautiful woman who was devoted to the goddess Artemis and sworn to perpetual virginity. But her father wanted her to marry, and she was much sought after, so she agreed to challenge each of her suitors to a footrace. If the suitor lost, he would be executed, which of course would be a bummer for him. But on the other hand, if he won, she would marry him. Many men were executed in the attempt to win Atalanta in marriage. But then along came Hippomenes, who had shown the forethought of asking Aphrodite for help. She gave him three golden apples, and once the race started and Hippomenes began falling behind, he tossed a golden apple out ahead of Atalanta, a little ways off the path. She veered away to pick it up, and Hippomenes took the lead. She overtook him again, and once more he tossed an apple. This happened three times, and in the end Atalanta was beaten. (And then in a surprise ending they both got turned into lions, but that's another part of the story.)

We women are running a race, and just like with Atalanta there are bright, shiny diversions being tossed out in an attempt to distract us and keep us from attaining our goal. I happen to think that the role of women is massively important and incredibly fundamental to the mission God has given us, and if *I* were the devil I would definitely make the goal of distracting the women one of my primary objects. Taking the women out of the running would be a spectacular way of undermining the entire mission of the church. And in our society, women are offered *multiple* opportunities of galloping away from the path after something that is simply there to sidetrack us and make us lose our focus. As mentioned before, some women take themselves out of the game in pursuit of some kind of fanciful escapism, but certainly not all women do that. Some may be enticed away by the lure of getting to live in the imaginary world of a fictional past, but many, many more are enticed away by the glitter of the real world and the promise of "fulfillment." This is the particular lie of our own age, and like all especially poisonous lies, it derives its power from having a bit of truth mixed in. The women who are tempted to retreat into imaginary worlds are kind of, by definition and by intention, living on the fringes of society. One of the reasons they are driven into an escapist approach is their own disenchantment with what they see around them, and their withdrawal from mainstream society is usually a very conscious decision. But the much bigger and much more prevailing problem of our time is that of women who are distracted away from their callings as women by the secular lies that surround us day in and day out, and the messages that constantly inundate us from our unbelieving and heavily individualistic society.

Just run this thought experiment. Two women, both thirty years old. One is a successful lawyer, single, well dressed, with a glamorous social life and a gorgeous apartment in the city. The other is married with three small children, making dinners for the family every night and dealing with laundry and carpool and messes. Put those two women in any movie, any TV show, any book—any story whatsoever. Who is living the fulfilled life? Who is doing important stuff? Who is a little bit pitiable and a bit of an also-ran? Who feels silly at her high school reunion? Who is "working" and who isn't? Obviously this is a no-brainer. We have all been conditioned to think that one of those women is fulfilling her dreams and the other one has "settled." One is doing big important things and the other . . . well, why did she bother getting a college degree again? Oh, I suppose maybe someday she'll go back to work . . .

Our society has this so ingrained that it's almost impossible *not* to think this way. Women who stay at home with their children will answer the question, "Do you work?" with an embarrassed, "No . . . not anymore. I studied business in school and someday I'd like to go back to work . . . "

Sometimes these women get a pat on the head—maybe in a country song which in essence says something like, "You may feel like your life isn't important but look at what a sweet guy I am because I still think you're hot." And we've been so conditioned to having the role of wife and mother actively despised that we think that's a really flattering message.

Our culture has worked diligently and tirelessly for well over a century to maneuver the chess board into its current setup. Feminism has wormed its way so deeply into our cultural consciousness that we see women as having only two main options in front of them. Women in our society may choose Option A (fulfilling career) or Option B (wife and mother). If you pick A, then you may go have a happy and fulfilled life; you get an education, pursue your dreams, make a lot of money, and you choose not to be tied down by a man or by children until *you* decide that they are what you need to complete your portfolio of a successful life.

On the other hand, if you pick Option B . . . we raise our eyebrows. We all know that you've just decided to waste your education, waste your abilities, waste your opportunities, and generally we all just think you're pitiful. Even the very women who themselves have chosen Option B often still feel like they're being left out of the big stuff. Many of them resent it. Many blame their husbands or their kids for the fact that they've wasted themselves. But this is because we have all been trained to see a career and an independent, successful life as *fulfillment*. Anything that gets in the way of fulfillment is taking something away from you—robbing you of what could have been a glorious and glamorous existence.

Occasionally a few superwomen manage to carve out for themselves a culturally acceptable third option. Such a superwoman has managed to become a wife and a mother, but has organized it in such a way that the husband and kids don't interfere with her life plans. She continues to pursue her career, and her husband and children simply fend for themselves in her wake as best they may. The kids are outsourced to a daycare or a nanny, the husband obviously shouldn't be allowed to stand in the way of her dreams, so he can just step aside. Our society has clearly ruled that when it comes down to a choice between your husband and children on the one side and *you* on the other . . . the right choice, the noble choice, the wise choice, is always *you*. You do what makes *you* happy. You do what makes *you* fulfilled. You don't let anyone get in the way of your dreams. You don't settle. You deserve it. You go girl!

This is the logic of the abortion industry. If that baby is going to get in the way of your dreams or your pursuits, then obviously that baby must be eliminated. Nothing must stand in the way of your aspirations. Your personal hopes, desires, or opportunities trump all else, and sacrificing your dreams for someone else is not seen as noble, it's seen as ludicrous. If you lay down your "life" for another, you certainly won't get respect or admiration from our society, and you will definitely get disdain. By many, your choice will just be seen as downright offensive. This overwhelming cultural peer pressure can be a large part of what dupes many women into accepting abortion as a solution to "a problem." Promised a quick fix, the sad reality is that these women can often suffer from the emotional damage of their choice for the rest of their lives.

But the truth is, the insistence on "the *right* to abortion on demand" is really nothing more than a glorification of simple selfishness. Our culture has tried to make a virtue of grabbiness, and has tried to bestow dignity upon an elbow-throwing, "me-first," yelling approach to life. We've tried to say that this is not only the road to success and fulfillment, it's also the noble choice. Unfortunately for us, however, a country full of individuals putting their own interests ahead of others is a culture that cannot possibly move forward in any productive way. Take a badly behaved third grade class fighting over a bowl of candy while the teacher is out of the room, and you have a very good idea of not only the success but also the dignity of this particular approach.

But the logic of the gospel is always the other way around. The way up is down. The road to promotion is to go to the back of the line. Sacrifice, laying down your own life, is at the very center of our faith. You want to save your life? Then you need to lose it. If you grab and grasp, you're guaranteed that it will slip through your fingers.

Christ's teaching on this was incredibly simple, but nonetheless intensely difficult for us to get our heads around. He tells us that he who wants to be first should be last, and that all sounds very spiritual and godly in theory . . . but at the moment when the rubber hits the road it suddenly doesn't make any sense to us at all. When you badly want to be at the front of the line, it really, really feels like what makes the most sense is to shove your way to the front. If our goal is to get to the front, and Christ points us toward the back—that's when we pull up short and say, "But wait! You don't understand the situation! If I go that way, I'll be at the back of the line! The *back,* you understand! I don't want the back—I'm aiming for the front!" But this is the gospel logic. Christ doesn't tell us that it's bad to be at the front—after all, He's giving us instructions on how to get there. The front of the line is where we're supposed to be aiming—but the road to get there is a surprising one.

That's why it's important to see all of this "fulfillment" nonsense as the fairy tale it is. Women who have chosen themselves at every turn in life, who have grasped, who have shoved others aside, who have put their own interests first in every endeavor, who are unable to even fathom the idea of submitting their desires to something outside of themselves . . . these are not happy women. *Those who try to save their lives will lose it.* Those who grab at "fulfillment" will never realize it. But those who are willing to lay that down, to put others ahead of themselves, to sacrifice themselves—those are the women who will truly find fulfillment. It's not that

Christ doesn't want you to experience fulfillment in your calling—it's that He *does*. In fact, we Christians are the only ones who can speak of the glorious truth of "calling" in the first place. We know that God has created us for a particular purpose—and since we trust that He knows what He's doing, it follows that when we're doing that which we were created for, we will be in our sweet spot. The world doesn't acknowledge the Creator, and therefore in place of "calling" they are left simply with "work." Ultimately all possibility of true, objective satisfaction in their work vanishes as well. Nothing but empty ambition remains. So don't fall for the lies the world tells us about how we can expect to achieve satisfaction. Putting yourself first is not actually the way to get there.

And I do think that we, as a culture, actually know this. One of the reasons that I think we tell ourselves the fulfillment story so often is that we're trying to convince ourselves of the truth of it. Have you ever done something that you knew was just plain wrong, but you're too embarrassed to actually put it right? Let's say that you told a lie, and there's just no getting around it—but you're not willing to go back and confess it to the person you were talking to. So there you are. What do you do? You try retelling the story in your head. You massage the facts a bit, trying to recreate the scene in such a way that what you said wasn't *actually* a lie. You tell yourself the story over and over, trying it out from different angles, trying to convince yourself that you weren't really in the wrong. But do you *ever* do that with conversations where you were completely fine and there was no problem? Of course not. The only time that you tell yourself something over and over and over is when you're trying to win the approval of your own conscience. I think that this is exactly what we are doing as a society. Movie after movie, TV show after TV show, is telling us that women who pursue their dreams and don't get sucked down by "domesticity" are the ones who are the heroic, the noble, the role models. And I think we know better, but we're not willing to admit our wrong, so we keep telling ourselves the story again and again.

Those are the two main distractions that are derailing Christian women and making us ineffective and irrelevant to the good kind of cultural transformation. We either shut our eyes to the mayhem around us and refuse to step outside our personal happy place, living the *Anne of Green Gables* dream, or we simply drift along with our culture and allow our ideals and our goals to be shaped by the unbelieving mainstream. The interesting part is that in both of these cases, we women are the ones doing it to ourselves. We don't live in a culture where the men won't let us speak and where we aren't allowed any freedom. Quite the contrary. If we feel like doing something, we actually live in a time and a place where we can go ahead and do it. Other Christian women in other centuries have struggled to fulfill their roles because they were being legitimately oppressed by tyrannical and unbiblical cultural norms—but we aren't struggling with that. If we fall for secular lies, that's on us. If we crawl away into a corner and try and live in a sweetsie, escapist, imaginary world, that's on us.

We have an awful lot of us Christian women in this country, and the road of feminine obedience is wide open. Not only that, we've stayed off of it for so long it is now completely unguarded. I believe that if we women decided, as a group, to take that road, we would knock a serious dent in the side of our culture's rebellion. But the truth is, a movement of women doing this wouldn't be terribly exciting or sexy. It wouldn't involve marches or protests or petitions or lobbying or t-shirts or fun runs. It would involve a lot of women manning their own separate battle stations in their own lives, in their own families, in the day-to-day grind. It would involve disciplining ourselves in the small, seemingly inconsequential areas of our lives—what we admire, what we try to get good at, what we strive for, what we prioritize, what we love. It would involve faithfulness, obedience, and sacrifice. It wouldn't seem like much. But one thing we know is that God loves to use the seemingly trivial things to accomplish staggering results. We may each feel like an insignificant little drop of water, and it may seem like the direction we take in our day-to-day lives doesn't make any difference to anyone. But when all the drops of water move the same way, what is more powerful and unstoppable than a wave?

SECTION TWO

ENTER FEMINISM

This idea that a stay-at-home mom is a sellout has become almost a catechism, and it has shaped our cultural consciousness so strongly that it has even managed to seep its way into the so-called conservative camp. Average, stay-at-home moms are a dwindling breed—but even those who have actually made the choice to accept that role can easily be made to feel insecure and ashamed about their lives. And many of the more public figures who are themselves supposedly brash and outspoken *opponents* of feminism are apparently insecure enough about this particular situation that they seem to be unable to engage in discussion with feminists without saying something like, "You can see that my critique of feminism is informed and valid because I myself am a very accomplished career woman." They are, apparently, worried that they won't be taken seriously unless they are waving an impressive resume around like a pom-pom while they talk. For instance, I lately ran across a book review written by a conservative woman for a conservative website, presumably addressing a conservative audience, and the article was attacking a recently released feminist book. The author of the piece was articulate, funny, and perceptive, and she delivered a fairly devastating critique of said book. And yet, in the course of the article she was very careful to let us know not once but several times, in clever and witty ways, that she herself is a successful career woman. She knows how the game is played. No one listens to you unless you have proven yourself in the business world—so you have to trot out your employment history and assure everyone that you're not one of those (heaven forbid) "domestic" women. Then, having established credibility, you may proceed to critique feminism.

But this makes as much sense as a woman donning a bikini, high heels, and a tiara to criticize the objectification of women in beauty pageants—because she's worried that if she doesn't, then no one will pay attention to her argument or take her seriously. I find it interesting that a man may legitimately object to feminism on philosophical grounds without once bringing his personal career success into the discussion. But a woman, apparently, is unable to discuss the subject at all without first establishing her street cred in the business world. And the trouble with this approach is that it grants victory to the feminists no matter which way you look at it. Heads they win; tails you lose. If you attack feminism and you *aren't* a career woman, you're dismissed out of hand—because why on earth would anyone take you seriously? If you attack feminism but you first make sure to point out that you aren't one of those oppressed, old-fashioned women, sucked down in the bog of domesticity . . . well, whatever comes out of your mouth next doesn't matter. You've ceded the whole game to the feminists already.

Whether we agree with it or not, we have all been shaped, more than we perhaps realize, by this particular narrative that housewives are brainless. To illustrate, try for a moment to picture in your mind's eye an impressive and accomplished woman who happens to be a critic of feminism, one who is educated, talented, outspoken, and articulate. A rare creature, I know, but just try to conjure up a mental picture of that woman. Now what does your imaginary woman look like? My guess is that you are imagining someone who looks and dresses like a journalist, wearing her pencil skirt, stilettos, and fake eyelashes in an office in Manhattan. Or maybe you've envisioned a very academic looking older woman in glasses and a brown jacket who teaches at a university—and not, in fact, a woman nursing a baby with a load of laundry that needs to be folded and a tray of cookies in the oven. Why is that? Why do we automatically assume that the woman at home with toddlers couldn't possibly have valid, insightful, or profound opinions, or that, if she does by some miracle have them, she's shamelessly wasting them by staying at home?

Why is it that for a woman to be taken "seriously" she has to keep her motherhood or her domesticity far away from the public eye like the crazy wife in *Jane Eyre* who is kept locked in the attic? (She's there, but she's embarrassing, so we try to not ever let anyone see her.) How did it come about that our obviously natural, creational, biological role as women has become an awkward disqualification from being a respectable human? A role that, if we can't shake off completely, we must at least have the decency to keep distant and mostly invisible? At some point, American motherhood became reduced to one of those brainless, menial jobs that no college graduate should ever have to demean themselves by accepting.

But a woman raising her children is not only shaping the next generation, she is also shaping little humans who are going to live forever. The souls she gave birth to are immortal. *Immortal.* And somehow, our culture looks at a woman who treats that as if it might be an important task and says, "It's a shame she's wasting herself. She could be doing something *important*—like filing paperwork for insurance claims."

How did we get to this point? Pardon the fly-by history lesson, but in order to understand where we're standing at the moment we need to glance back a couple of centuries and try to identify the point at which we jumped the tracks.

3.

PROTO-FEMINISM

The earliest of the feminists can actually be traced all the way back to Britain during Jane Austen's lifetime, when Mary Wollstonecraft first appeared on the horizon in 1759, a cloud no bigger than a man's fist. This is hugely important to note: Feminism did not spring up, armed and dangerous, in the 1960s when Gloria Steinem started making headlines—actually, by the time that abortion was legalized in America, feminism was close on two hundred years old. This is important because far too often conservatives want to reject the unsavory fruits of feminism without ever pausing to wonder about the orchard where the fruit was cultivated. They are like dissatisfied movie watchers who, offended by the distasteful final scene in the film, want to rewind it five minutes and then try again, hoping for a different outcome "this time." No, that final scene is what the whole plot has been building up to; it's not an anomaly. And in the same way, we women of the twenty-first century find ourselves standing in the ruins of the West, but this is no recent accident—it is the logical conclusion of the last several hundred years.

Mary Wollstonecraft led a somewhat unconventional life by eighteenth-century standards. An intellectually inclined woman living in the heyday of the Enlightenment, she was a member of a group of radical thinkers and artists centered around Joseph Johnson, publisher of the periodical called *Analytical Review,* which was known for its revolutionary political and religious ideas. She pursued a love affair with a fellow member of the group, a married artist, and in 1790 she published *A Vindication of the Rights of Men* supporting the Revolution in France. She followed it up soon after with *A Vindication of the Rights of Woman* (1792), now considered to be one of the first philosophical treatises on feminism, although she never used that word, since it was yet to be coined and would not become widely used until nearly a century later. Soon after the publication of *A Vindication of the Rights of Woman*, she traveled to France, arriving shortly before the Reign of Terror began in earnest. An ardent supporter of the Revolution, she remained in France for the duration, and during that time gave birth to an illegitimate child by an American who eventually abandoned her. After the Revolution ended, she returned home to England with her daughter and several times attempted suicide because her lover refused to take her back. Eventually she met and became pregnant by another man, a radical thinker and philosopher named William Godwin who, among other things, rejected the idea of marriage. The two decided to marry anyway, however, so that the child would be legitimate, but the couple moved into two houses next door to each other so that they could each keep their independence. In 1797, she gave birth and then died of complications just over a week later.

That daughter, named Mary after her mother, was raised in Godwin's household and given an impressive, although obviously radical, education. Part of Godwin's philosophy was the idea of free love and a rejection of traditional sexual norms. In pursuance of this philosophy, at the age of sixteen, Mary Godwin became the lover of Percy Bysshe Shelley, the (then married) romantic poet. The couple left Shelley's wife (pregnant with her second child) at home in England and traveled to Switzerland together, and when they returned, Mary too was pregnant. That baby died, but Mary shortly became pregnant again and gave birth to a second child. Several months later, the couple returned to Switzerland and spent the summer at Lake Geneva with Lord Byron. It was during this summer (unnaturally darkened by ash from a volcanic eruption in Chile, by the way) that she began writing the novel *Frankenstein*. She was eighteen years old. Later that same year, Shelley's wife killed herself, and three weeks later Shelley married Mary.

4.

FIRST-WAVE FEMINISM

Across the ocean in 1820—just two years after the publication of Mary Shelley's *Frankenstein* and a mere twenty-three years after the death of her mother, Mary Wollstonecraft—Susan B. Anthony was born. If Wollstonecraft was a lone, early tremor, Anthony was one of those who helped usher in the earthquake in earnest. First-wave feminism is typically seen as stretching from the nineteenth through the early twentieth centuries, and since it was an enormous movement, there were obviously many, many influential women involved. Anthony, however, was one of the well-known champions of the movement and is now considered a hero by very nearly everyone, so it's worth taking a look at what she fought for.

Susan B. Anthony was born in Massachusetts into a Quaker family, although by the end of her life she was thoroughly agnostic. By the time she had reached her late teens she was already involved in the abolitionist movement, but much of her life was devoted to the twin causes of women's suffrage (the right to vote) and the temperance movement (the criminalization of alcohol). Although she was not present at the famous Seneca Falls Convention in 1848 (the historic, first-ever women's rights convention), she soon after became good friends with one of the organizers, Elizabeth Cady Stanton, and the two grew to be very nearly inseparable. Anthony lived in the Stanton household much of the time, but since Stanton was married with seven children and Anthony remained single, it was Anthony who had the freedom to travel, speak, and do much of the legwork involved in mobilizing the feminist movement. Stanton was the intellectual behind the scenes who did much of the writing; Anthony was the organizer, speaker, and a bit more of the public face. Stanton herself famously said of Anthony, "I forged the thunderbolts, she fired them." Their partnership was incredibly influential, and the two were largely involved in the passage of three amendments to the Constitution. In the midst of the Civil War, the two women founded the Women's Loyal National League, the first women's political organization on a national scale. They founded the league in order to campaign for an amendment outlawing slavery, and managed to collect almost 400,000 signatures for their petition. Immediately after the close of the war, the amendment was passed.

The next major campaign for the two women was the fight for women's suffrage as well as the battle to enact prohibition. For the first-wave feminists, these two issues were inseparable. The Women's Christian Temperance Union, which was largely responsible for the Eighteenth Amendment (Prohibition), was also a huge supporter of the suffrage movement, and at the same time, all the suffragettes were deeply involved in the temperance movement. In fact, Anthony and Stanton had formed the Women's State Temperance Society and had been lobbying to prohibit the sale of alcohol in New York State a full decade before the outbreak of the Civil War.

Years ago, at a yard sale, I found an old temperance song booklet, obviously intended for use at temperance meetings. I bought it, of course, because how could anyone pass up something as awesome as that? The music to every song has a serious marching band feel to it, and the link between suffrage and temperance is illustrated magnificently by the lyrics from one of the songs:

> But if the men can't drive it out we'll call for women voters;
> they'll scrub out the nation's barber shop with all the whiskey
>> bloaters.
> When we get women voters, good-by to beer keg toters.
> O-ho! O-ho! When we get women voters.[1]

The Eighteenth Amendment went into effect in 1920, and that same year the Nineteenth Amendment was ratified, giving women the right to vote. Neither Stanton nor

---

1. Dr. J. B. Herbert, *The Live Wire* (Chicago: The Rodeheaver Co.) No. 8.

Anthony were alive to see it, but their tireless and impressive efforts for these two causes were enormously responsible for these eventual twin victories for feminism.

These women had been fighting for the right of women to vote in general. But in particular, one of the most pressing issues that the women wanted to vote *on* was the issue of alcohol. It is interesting that the circle of radicals around Wollstonecraft in England had been advocating for the rights of women and the idea of free love and the rejection of traditional sexual norms. In America, the rights of women were being fought for by teetotalers who wanted to criminalize alcohol. Those are two groups who, you would imagine, couldn't possibly have a lot in common. However, America eventually caught up with its progressive cousins across the Atlantic, and it wasn't terribly long before the feminists in America began talking about sex as well. It's inescapable, really, because nothing is more likely to drop an anchor on a woman's career as thoroughly as having children, which, it must be noted, is the obvious result of sex.

If you glance back through the basic biographical details of the women we have just discussed, children are a hugely defining plot point in each of their lives. Wollstonecraft and Godwin acted against their own stated beliefs by getting married—and this was because they had to think of their child who would be the one to suffer the stigma attached to illegitimacy. Mary then died young, at age thirty-eight, because of complications in childbirth. In her case, not only did pregnancy influence her marriage, it also caused her death. Her daughter, Mary Shelley, a promising intellect living in accord with the radical ideas of free love, was twice a mother, as well as having to deal with the emotional baggage of losing a baby, by the time she was eighteen. Elizabeth Cady Stanton, although a highly educated and gifted speaker and writer, was also a mother of seven, and therefore unable to travel and speak because of her duties at home. Susan B. Anthony, although not as educated or as intellectually gifted as Stanton, had the advantage of being unmarried and childless, and therefore possessed much more freedom to pursue her career, changing the world by delivering the speeches that Stanton had written for her. We can't help but ask ourselves if that's the reason her face is on the coin instead of Stanton's. Is being childless a bigger advantage to a woman than being gifted, smart, or educated? Are children the bushel under which women are forced to hide their light? Apparently so. If women wanted to pursue successful, intellectual careers, they needed to *not* have children . . . and this meant they needed to remain married to their work, maintain a celibate existence, and have nothing to do with men. Nuns renounce sex to become "married to Christ"; the early feminists had to renounce sex in order to be wed to their careers.

On the other hand . . . what if there was a work-around? What if women could divorce themselves from their fertility, maintain their career advantage of remaining childless, and yet have the freedom to pursue a Wollstonecraftesque lifestyle of free love, but without the consequences? True women's liberation would have been achieved—liberation from children and the duties they entail, liberation from the natural consequences of sex, and inevitably, liberation from the restrictions of traditional sexual morality. Enter Margaret Sanger, preaching this gospel of liberation. Before her crusade for birth control, men were technically free to indulge in as much immorality as they wanted without it ever necessarily having adverse affects on their careers. But women, on the other hand, were unable to live with the same "freedom" as men in this regard without it necessarily ending in a baby that the woman was then left to take care of. Within the confines of traditional marriage, both the man and the woman are deeply affected by the birth of a baby, and the burden of caring for and raising the child falls heavily on the father. But outside of marriage, the consequences fall on the woman alone. Outside of marriage, a man could, potentially, father large numbers of children without ever even knowing of their existence—the same is, obviously, not true of women. A woman cannot be a mother without it upending her entire life.

The feminists did, and still do, view this as deeply unfair. In the early twentieth century, a woman could get married and have children, and she might have the security of knowing that the father was equally invested in the care of the children, but she was also then tied to her husband, to her home, to her children, and was unable to experience the freedom of a career. On the other hand, if she remained single in the interests of freedom or career success, she also had to remain celibate if she wanted to avoid the complications of children—and this same either-or dilemma was not true for the men.

Sanger was the woman who changed all that. She was another of the first-wave feminists, and she was born in 1879, when Susan B. Anthony was seventy-three years old. The right to vote was not won until Sanger was forty-one years old, and she by that time was already well embarked on her crusade to bring birth control and "safe" abortions to American women. Her first clinic (which was later to become Planned Parenthood) opened its doors in 1916, four years before suffrage was achieved. Notice that even before women had the right to vote, abortion was already a key component of the vision to liberate women—it was not an afterthought in the 70s. Emancipation for women was seen as emancipation from the restrictions of biology—essentially emancipation from their own bodies.

Sanger was the daughter of an atheist socialist, and she herself became involved in the radical leftist politics of the pre-World War I Greenwich Village set. It was at this point that America seems to have finally caught up to where England had been a century before—with a philosophical *avant-garde* arguing for socialism and free love. Sanger's main crusade was to bring birth control to American women, but it was born out of her belief that a woman must assume absolute control over her own fertility and that motherhood should be "voluntary." Even though legalized abortion was not her particular fight, she had no ethical problems with abortion, and the crusade to legalize it was very much the logical phase two of the war she was waging. Planned Parenthood, the organization that she founded and remained involved with for fifty years, is today the single largest provider of abortions in America—and this is no accident. Given her belief that pregnancy is not something that "should just happen to you," the ability to prevent *or end* a pregnancy is vital to her vision of women being liberated from the tyranny of reproduction. Given her premises, the right to abortion is an absolute necessity.

In 1936, after years of campaigning, numerous arrests, and multitudes of newsletters and publications called things like *The Woman Rebel*, Sanger won a court battle that had the effect of making birth control more accessible to American women. Because of her interest in the whole question of reproduction, or more specifically the lack thereof, she was also an advocate for eugenics and the enforced sterilization of the unfit.

It's worth noting that she was an advocate for this at a moment in history when eugenics was not just a hypothetical theory to be speculated about in classrooms, but a bloody and vicious experiment in the midst of being carried out in Germany—an experiment that several hundred thousand American men gave their lives to stop. For Sanger, the chief end of birth control was to maximize the number of births from the "fit" and minimize the number of births from the "unfit." So, in her view, birth control didn't just liberate individual women, it also benefited the human race by preventing the births of those who would be considered dysgenic, or detrimental to the ideal society. She lived to see her victory in the birth control department, but she died in 1966, seven years before *Roe v. Wade.*

5.

PSYCHOTROPICS AND
SECOND-WAVE FEMINISM

When I was a kid in the late 80s, my mom had a subscription to *Better Homes and Gardens* magazine, and it's hard to think of a magazine more quintessentially geared toward wives and moms. Full of articles on home decorating, gardening, and recipes, this was not a magazine being marketed to male stockbrokers or lumberjacks. It was clearly aimed at a very particular demographic. I remember looking through the magazines when they arrived every month, and oddly the only thing I really remember about them was that in every single issue there was always a prominent, full page ad for Virginia Slims cigarettes. The ads stood out in a way, because the rest of the magazine wasn't about fashion at all, but the Virginia Slims page would always feature a large picture of some terribly stylish woman. I remember always pausing on those pages, studying the ad and trying to figure it out. My elementary school self didn't understand the larger social point, but I clearly remember how each one of the ads was staged. Front and center would be the model, looking well dressed and confident, hair blowing in the breeze, cigarette in hand, and in the background were what appeared to be old sepia-toned photographs of turn-of-the-century women, having a rotten time and generally being afflicted by their husbands in some way. They were maybe struggling with hogsheads and washboards while their husband wore slippers and smoked a pipe and read the paper. Or the woman in a bonnet was shoveling her way through a snowy field to make a path for her husband to walk on. Or he would be in his dressing gown, toasting his self-satisfied, privileged little toes in front of the fire while she staggered in from the snow with a load of firewood. As she hung clothes on the line, some little caption would read something like, "Mr. Lee Evans made it clear that he wore the pants in the family, but once a week he didn't mind giving them to his wife." The scenes of male oppression in the sepia-tone photos changed, and the outfits on the stylish model changed, but the basic set-up was always the same. Then across the front of everything was the caption, "You've come a long way, baby."[1]

The message was hardly subtle. Each and every Virginia Slims ad was a tribute to the victories of feminism and a testimonial to the liberation of women from the tyranny of

---

1. The quoted lines are from a 1991 Virginia Slims ad.

domesticity. So how is it that a magazine for homemakers (and hardly an edgy or controversial magazine) could have an ad every single month advertising a product to homemakers based on the premise of *despising* homemaking? The ads were comic, sure. But the point that was simply assumed was that the women of the past were silly, weak, downtrodden, afflicted, and living petty lives. Every ad reinforced the narrative that homemaking was a dead end—a soul-sucking, demeaning, humiliating job. But now! Now that we are women of the 80s with incredible bangs, we can roller-skate and do jazzercise and smoke cigarettes and generally whoop it up because we have *jobs!* and have freed ourselves from the tyranny of the men.

My childhood was spent in a decade during which our society simply assumed the truth of all that, but it was actually during my mother's childhood that this message had become mainstreamed. The first-wave feminists, so radical in their time, had apparently done their job well. They had won their victories and laid the foundation upon which the second-wave feminists of the 1960s were able to build.

World War II and the decade which followed it were essentially the intermission between the two waves of feminism. Although the feminists had been hard at work for a century and more, their true victories were not achieved until the era between the World Wars. But their momentum was lost with the advent of the Second World War. World War I ended in 1918. In 1920 Prohibition was enacted (victory number one) and suffrage was achieved (victory number two), and in 1936 Sanger had accomplished the first of her successes in the larger goal of bringing reproductive freedom to women (victory number three). The primary aims of the first-wave feminists had become reality. But in 1941, a mere five years after Sanger's birth control success, the US entered the war in Europe, which drastically changed the face of America.

The effects of World War II on America are fascinating, but much too big a subject to get into here. Suffice it to say that in the 1950s, the role of women suffered a bit of a relapse from the trajectory that it had appeared to be on before the war. The massive economic growth, the technological advances, the baby boom, the advent of suburbia, were all phenomena that shaped our country profoundly. Seemingly a decade of wholesome family values, family vacations in station wagons to go visit the National Parks, *I Love Lucy* and *Leave it to Beaver* on TV, and high school students wearing letterman jackets and poodle skirts at sock hops, the 50s can feel, in retrospect, idyllic.

And yet, in 1963, a woman named Betty Friedan published a book called *The Feminine Mystique*,[2] in which she took a hatchet to the notion that American women were living in a time of wholesome bliss. The book was a massive success, and its publication is generally seen as the kick-off of second-wave feminism. The book was basically an articulation of the listlessness and unfulfilled dreariness felt

---

2. Betty Friedan, *The Feminine Mystique* (New York: W.W. Norton, 1963).

by the women of my grandmother's generation who were married with children, and were nonetheless still unhappy. The mainstream society of 1950s, post-war America had held that a woman's goal should be to marry and have children—so why, a decade later, did all those women who had achieved that goal actually feel like they had been ripped off? Friedan tapped into a very deep vein of discontent among American housewives, and the book caught like wildfire. Friedan described the pitiable plight of the housewife, forever shackled to her merely biological role—that of childbearing—and not able to find fulfillment or meaning in higher, more challenging pursuits. She described the *ennui* felt by American wives and mothers in great detail and called it "the problem that has no name"—a sensation of listlessness, boredom, and lack of purpose coupled with the haunting fear that life is passing you by. Much of the strength of her argument lay in the fact that she was assuring her readers that they were not alone, that millions of other women felt exactly the same way. Women grabbed onto this idea *en masse*, with all the relieved enthusiasm of someone finding out that all their aches and pains are actually a genuine medical condition—and not only that, a condition that has a treatment.

The condition, in this case, was the *feminine mystique*, and Friedan's proposed solution was that women as a group needed to see what was happening to them, listen and respond to that nagging discontent, and essentially take the next step in their evolution: "In a sense that goes beyond any woman's life, I think this is a crisis of women growing up—a turning point from an immaturity that has been called femininity to full human identity."[3] Notice that. From immaturity to full human identity. And what was the immaturity? It was femininity itself. Women needed to leave behind the feminine in order to become fully human. And of course once this premise is granted, then by definition we must look back at those turn-of-the-century women, or women who embraced traditionally feminine roles, as less developed, less intelligent, less evolved, and honestly, less human. Looking *back* at those women necessarily involves looking *down* on them.

The mere fact that her book was so successful shows us that America was full of disillusioned, disenchanted, and unhappy wives (it wasn't the men buying her book, after all), and the widespread, enthusiastic response in some sense vindicated her argument.[4] Have you ever noticed how babies get extremely cranky just before they make some new developmental leap? Just before they can sit up they get all fussy and difficult—as if they know they're missing something. Then one day they learn to sit up and lo! all is right in the world again. Until just before they crawl. Then they get all chippy again until they figure out the crawling thing. Friedan was essentially just diagnosing the

---

3. Friedan, *Feminine Mystique*, 80.

4. When I say that her book was a hit, I am not exaggerating. For six weeks *The Feminine Mystique* was on the *New York Times* Best Seller list, and the first paperback printing sold 1.4 million copies.

indisputable widespread discontent of American women as that same phenomenon. They needed to develop. They needed to take the next step, and then happiness would follow. Her answer, her solution to the feminine mystique, lay in the opportunity for a career outside the home. A woman's identity should not be found solely in her role as procreator and tidier-upper of the home; she needed to achieve self-actualization by leaving all that behind and striving for something more.

That message was incredibly dynamic in the 60s, and it became so universally accepted that by the time of the 80s you could not only simply assume the truth of it, you could also joke about it in the extremely uncontroversial pages of *Better Homes and Gardens.* Furthermore, you could do so confidently, knowing that you would make money off the ad when you ran it there.

There seems to be no doubt that Friedan was on to something. The women in America were truly miserable in their 1950s housewifey roles. However, that may well be a difficult concept to get our heads around because it's so contrary to the common depictions of the decade, most of which seem very vintagey and quaint and squeaky clean and June Cleaver-ish. We tend to want to look at the 50s as that moment when America was happy and healthy and wholesome—before the radical 60s bundled us all into the handbasket and launched us on our journey to Hell. But I think if we look at a parallel example we'll see this a bit more clearly. Have you ever seen a marriage blow up completely when no one on the outside had suspected any-thing was wrong? You know, the kind of sad incident where a picture-perfect, model church-going family suddenly has a meltdown and surprises everyone? The universal truth in such situations is that the problems in that marriage go back much further than the moment when all the friends found out about it. In such cases everyone discovers that for the last four (or forty!) years, that family had been smiling sweetly at church and devouring each other at home. The moment when the wife finally snaps and leaves her husband is not the first moment in which she became unhappy. In a similar way, the widespread cultural rejection of traditional femininity in the 60s should show us that the resentment had been building for a while. Certainly not every single housewife in the 50s was unhappy, but it's valid to recog-nize that the vitriol of the 60s came from somewhere and did not spring up *ex nihilo*. When the women of the 60s loudly announced, "We hate this; we're burning it down," I think it's fair for us to assume that they hated it, and also that they wanted to burn it down. The seeds of our current feminism, therefore, go back farther than Friedan and her theories about the feminine mystique. She never would have gotten traction with this argument unless the women of America were already eager, ready, almost des-perate to hear it!

So what on earth was going on with the women of the 50s? Why were they miserable? How could they have been so unhappy and so over it all? As I mentioned, Friedan thought she knew what was causing the problem, and in 1963 she proposed her solution to the unhappy women of America: What they needed was the opportunity to pursue careers outside the home and the liberty to leave behind their children and husbands in order to fulfill themselves. She submitted her hypothesis, the nation jumped on board, and for the past half century the experiment has been conducted. We're far enough into it now that it seems valid for us to survey the evidence and see if it turns out that Friedan was right. So: Are American women currently allowed to pursue their dreams in the workplace? Have they successfully freed themselves from the shackles of domesticity and motherhood? Are they now happier and more fulfilled than they were in the 50s?

The first question is easy enough to establish. According to the Department of Labor, women comprised 47 percent of the United States' workforce in 2010,[5] and in 2013, 57.2 percent of all American women were in the workforce. [6] This is a dramatic rise from the 22 percent employment rate of women in 1960.[7] It seems safe to say that in America today, women have the freedom to pursue careers if they so choose. And they usually so choose.

---

5. Department of Labor, "Women in the Labor Force in 2010," United States, http://www.dol.gov/wb/factsheets/qf-laborforce-10.htm (accessed Feb. 24, 2016).

6. Department of Labor, "Latest Annual Data: Women of Working Age," United States, http://www.dol.gov/wb/stats/latest_annual_data.htm (accessed Feb. 24, 2016).

7. Theresa Riley, "How America's Workforce has Changed Since 1960," http://billmoyers.com/2012/06/18/how-americas-workforce-has-changed-since-1960/ (accessed Feb. 24, 2016).

And what about being tied down to our merely biological role of procreating? Are women today having more children or fewer children than women of the 50s? According to the World Bank, the total fertility rate (or average number of children per woman) in America in 1960 was 3.65. There was a dramatic drop in the 60s, and by 1976 it had dropped down to 1.74—less than half of what it was a mere sixteen years earlier. That statistic has roughly hovered a little below 2 ever since.[8] There is no doubt that women today are less tied to motherhood than they were in the 50s. Margaret Sanger's dream has been realized, and most women of today think of motherhood as something that is absolutely voluntary and a condition over which they have complete control.

But has it made us happier? The problem with housewifery in the 50s (according to Friedan) was that it made women feel empty and sad. So are American women correspondingly happier now that we've shaken that off? Surely, if Friedan's hypothesis was correct, women should be dramatically happier now since we are dramatically *more* likely to have a career and dramatically *less* likely to have children.

Happiness is difficult to measure, of course. It's not like taking someone's temperature or measuring their height and weight. But one fairly tangible way of diagnosing the

8. Google, "Public Data: Fertility Rate," data from World Bank, https://www.google.com/publicdata/explore?ds=d5bncppjof8f9_&met_y=sp_dyn_tfrt_in&idim=country:USA:RUS:CAN&hl=en&dl=en (accessed Feb. 24, 2016).

overall cheerfulness factor of the population is by finding out how many of the general public are taking antidepressants. While that statistic isn't completely conclusive, it's surely enough to give us a rough idea of how generally happy or unhappy large groups of people are. Antidepressants proper had not been mainstreamed in the 50s, but there were plenty of medications that were being offered for the related maladies of anxiety, nerves, etc. And by 1963, 21 percent of American women were on one form or another of psychotropic medication.[9] Even Friedan herself talks about women trying to blot out their sorrows by resorting to tranquilizers. In fact, this is one of her supporting arguments to convince her readers of the seriousness of the problem. "Many suburban housewives were taking tranquilizers like cough drops. 'You wake up in the morning, and you feel as if there's no point in going on another day like this. So you take a tranquilizer because it makes you not care so much that it's pointless.'"[10] Popularly referred to as "mother's little helpers," these drugs were tangible evidence that, when Friedan claimed that women were unhappy, she was not making things up. Friedan's book came out in 1963, and three years later The Rolling Stones were

9. Tessa Johnson, "How to Be a Domestic Goddess," Wellcome History, https://wellcomehistory.wordpress.com/2013/02/25/how-to-be-a-domestic-goddess (accessed June 22, 2016). Only 9 percent of men were on psychotropic medication at the same time. There's similar data from a decade later (1973) as well: See Allan V. Horwitz, "How an Age of Anxiety Became an Age of Depression," *Milbank* Q. 2010 Mar; v. 88(1): 112–138. Available online at the US National Library of Medicine, http://www.ncbi.nlm.nih.gov/pmc/articles/PMC2888013 (accessed Feb. 25, 2016).

10. Friedan, *Feminine Mystique,* 31.

singing "Mother's Little Helper,"which said much the same thing as Friedan, but with a tune.

> Mother needs something today to calm her down
>
> And though she's not really ill
>
> There's a little yellow pill
>
> She goes running for the shelter of a mother's little helper
>
> And it helps her on her way, gets her through her busy day
>
> "Things are different today"
>
> I hear every mother say
>
> Cooking fresh food for a husband's just a drag
>
> So she buys an instant cake and she burns her frozen steak
>
> And goes running for the shelter of a mother's little helper
>
> And two help her on her way, get her through her busy day.[11]

It seems indisputable that an unhealthily large number women were truly miserable, and were medicating themselves for it on a rather massive scale.[12] But if Friedan was right, if the solution to this unhappiness was a chance to pursue careers outside the home and an ability to shake off the restrictions of motherhood, then surely the tireless efforts of the feminists for the past fifty years must have produced the promised fruit of happier and more fulfilled women. Surely we should see a significant drop in the use of mother's little helpers.

---

11. Mick Jagger and Keith Richards, "Mother's Little Helper," *Aftermath,* 1966.

12. For a much more complete and very interesting discussion of the prevalence of psychotropics in the 50s, see Chapters 2-5 on the history of the drug Miltown in *The Age of Anxiety: A History of America's Turbulent Affair with Tranquilizers* by Andrea Tone (New York: Basic Books, 2009).

But I'm afraid it didn't turn out like that. Women did not become correspondingly happier the further they got away from housewifery and motherhood. Use of psychotropic medications hasn't dwindled in the slightest but has rather increased. Today 26 percent of American women are unhappy enough to go see their doctor about it and get a prescription. In 1963, one in every five women was medicating her unhappiness, and today we're up to more than one in four women.[13] And women are more than two and a half times more likely to be on the medications than men.[14] Given women's mass pilgrimage from the domestic world to the corporate, perhaps we should start referring to those little yellow pills as "personal assistants."

So are women statistically more employed now than they were in Friedan's day? Documentably and resoundingly, yes. Are women less tied to their biological role? Documentably and resoundingly, yes. Has it brought us the happiness we were promised? Documentably and resoundingly, no. If we go purely on the basis of the prescription levels, women are even sadder now than they were then. I'm afraid that Friedan's thesis simply doesn't hold up. For the last fifty years, American women have chased the rainbow and the pot of happy has not turned up.

---

13. Medco Health Solutions, Inc., *America's State of Mind: A Report by Medco*, http://apps.who.int/medicinedocs/documents/s19032en/s19032en.pdf (accessed Feb. 24, 2016).

14. Peter Wehrwein, "Astounding increase in antidepressant use by Americans," Harvard Health Publications, http://www.health.harvard.edu/blog/astounding-increase-in-antidepressant-use-by-americans-201110203624 (accessed Feb. 24, 2016).

I can hear the objection already. "The unhappiness of women today has nothing to do with the fact that they are allowed to have careers. This is gross oversimplification, and there are many other factors involved." True. I grant that. But if that's the case, then surely it was an oversimplification when Friedan argued that it was housewifery that was the problem and careers were the solution?

In the big picture, looking back on the situation in the 1950s, it's obvious that our country desperately needed Christ. Widespread emptiness, purposelessness, and unhappiness are not marks of a culture that is godly and thriving. Women of the 50s didn't simply need careers, they needed grace—and the rest of the discussion that follows is by no means denying that principle or forgetting that it is the case. But since this is a book about the role of women in society, that's the subject we need to examine, and so we're going to zoom in past the overarching need that our country had for reformation and instead talk about what would have been the impact on the cultural role of women if that reformation had in fact happened. Let's say that during the 60s, instead of the sexual revolution that we actually had, there had been another Great Awakening. What impact would repentance have had on the role of women in the culture? If, in her misery and unhappiness, America had fallen to her knees instead of throwing herself into the pursuit of licentiousness, would there have been any resultant change in the way women were viewed? Absolutely there would have been. I would argue that one of the first things that we would have needed to chuck out the window would have been the idealistic, superficial, and incredibly shallow view of homemaking that was flourishing in the 50s.

Somewhere along the line, America had swallowed a poisonous lie about what women were for, and by the end of the 50s was starting to feel queasy—but it wasn't until the 60s that the vomiting started. It's not enough to look at the vomiting stage, recognize that this is unhelpful and problematic, and argue that we should rewind back to the part where we had eaten the bad oyster but hadn't started to feel it yet. If we, today, somehow managed to successfully recreate the 50s, we would also have unavoidably recreated the preconditions for the 60s. Those two decades are a package deal. Too often conservatives and liberals are fighting over a completely irrelevant issue when it comes to this. The liberals think the vomiting was necessary and helpful (pay no mind to the fact that our country is now in a high fever, quivering spastically on the floor, showing no signs of improvement) and the ultraconservatives argue that this whole situation is terrible, so let's go back to that idyllic and nostalgic day when we ate the bad oyster—and then eat it again. I sometimes think we need to shut both parties up in a closet somewhere and let them argue it out amongst themselves while we try to honestly assess the situation and hopefully come up with a better answer.

6.

WOMEN DISPOSSESSED

So what was wrong with the femininity of the 1950s? Why were women feeling so gutted and so purposeless? To answer that question we need to look past what was going on in individual homes and see the bigger picture of what was going on in America at that time. We need to figure out what went wrong—not so that we can sit around and criticize our grandmothers, but so that we can figure out how to spare our daughters.

There's no question that in the 50s, America hit an unprecedented level of prosperity. Money, progress, technology, standard of living—all of these categories skyrocketed. Leisure time, something which had previously belonged solely to the privileged wealthy, was suddenly possessed by the middle classes. America was going through a massive growth spurt and almost couldn't keep up with itself. Shock waves from this newfound prosperity of the middle class were felt across the entire culture in everything from architecture to what people ate for dinner and how they spent their weekends. One place where the changes were felt acutely was in the home. With the rise of suburbia, homes were new, modern, and efficient. With the explosion of technology and its suddenly increased availability, America's love affair with efficiency was brought into the home. The average household was rapidly equipped with electric ranges, refrigerators, electric mixers, vacuums, telephones, toasters, and hosts of other gadgets all geared toward creating a life of ease for the homemaker.

My husband grew up knowing his great-grandmother—a woman who lived through World War I, whose husband sent her letters from the front. As a child, my husband used to visit her out on the farm where she had lived since she was a young woman. He remembers getting drinks from the tin bucket at the well, and he remembers the fruit trees and her enormous garden, which yielded all the produce that she canned for the winter. Even into the 70s when her grandchildren and great-grandchildren came to visit, she would go out and wring the necks of a few chickens to fix for dinner and send the kids out to the garden to pick the beans. When she was a young wife, she would make angel food cakes (without the aid of an electric mixer— can you even imagine?) and take them into town to sell on the weekends to earn money. When we sit down with our kids to watch a movie on a Friday night, we curl up under quilts that she made—quilts made of flour sacks, old clothes, whatever came to hand. I love those quilts because they tell a story of a woman for whom quilting was a reality of life, not a cute thing she did on retreats with her girlfriends. These quilts are downright utilitarian, and they wear like iron. Some of the squares on them are cut from old shirts—buttons included. Some of the squares are wool, some cotton, and matching the colors was not the point. These blankets are the evidence of a woman determined to keep her family warm, and she used whatever she could scrounge to make that happen.

For a woman of that generation, being a homemaker was an enormous job. Massive. Getting your family through the winter was a big deal. Gardening, for a woman like her, wasn't just a hobby, it was crucially important. Those women had to work like crazy if they wanted to feed and clothe their families. Not only was the work incredibly difficult, it took skill, perseverance, and creativity. It also included the possibility of a huge amount of satisfaction in a job well done or devastating consequences of failure. It involved risk. These women were playing high-stakes poker, and they had to get good at it.

But then along came the next generation, and suddenly, almost without warning, life got easy. Getting through the winter wasn't really a fear. You didn't have to fill your cupboards with all the jars of produce you canned, you could just trot along to the store to buy a few tins of beans or corn. You want dinner? Pop a TV dinner into the oven—no need to go outside and chase down a chicken, much less kill, pluck, gut, and cook it. Your little boy needs a winter coat? Go down to the department store and buy him one—no need to pick apart your husband's old coat and remake it for a child. Problems that would have taken a woman of a previous generation a week to solve could now be fixed with a simple phone call to order something from a catalog.

In one sense, this sounds like the promised land for housewives! I mean, how is this not completely fabulous news? Obviously it is, mostly. But in another sense, you can feel how the possibility of satisfaction in your work was removed. Let's say that you were a woman living on a farm at the turn of the last century. You have a lot of kids and not a lot of money. Winter's coming, and you've got to feed them all the way through it. When do you start planning? The split minute you get through the last winter, that's when. You pull out the seeds you saved from last year's crop, you start your seeds, you plant your garden (and no, you can't rent a rototiller, so you probably have to fuss around with a hoe or a horse and plow or something). And don't forget that if that garden is going to feed the family it's going to have to be a rather massive—cute container gardening or interesting Pinterest-worthy novelty gardens would not cut it. You tend it all summer, and you harvest. You can, you dry, you preserve. You fill your root cellar and hopefully by midway through autumn you can stand back and survey the fruit of all that labor, grateful that it all came together and secure in the knowledge that you have supplied your family with what they need. Now compare that feeling with grabbing a can of beans at the store and feeling happy that you remembered to do that so there's some green on your kids' plates tonight. It's much easier, yes . . . but not quite the same in terms of satisfaction in a job well done.

All of the cultural expectations for women—expectations the women had for themselves—suddenly were quite easily attainable. It became simple to put dinner on the table, simple to keep the house, simple to clothe the family. The once-skilled labor of the women had suddenly been replaced by household gadgets and the availability of mass-produced goods. It's no wonder the women felt dispossessed. What at first must have seemed like heaven on earth must have very soon gotten boring. If you ever read advice for housewives of the 50s, it's so empty and flat and insipid that it's no wonder they were unhappy. *The ideal housewife must make sure the house is quiet and tidy before the husband comes home. The ideal housewife must have dinner on the table when he arrives. The ideal housewife must run a dust-cloth over the tables before her husband walks in the door. The ideal housewife should take care to have her hair tidy before he arrives.* Seriously? That's it? The *difficulty* of the work had been dealt with by the improvements in the standard of living, so there wasn't much left to do except stand around making sure there wasn't any dust on anything. One understands why, by the late 50s, the women felt like the work was demeaning—but I can't imagine Great-Grandma Hawkins feeling like her work was demeaning. Difficult, yes, but demeaning? She was working shoulder to shoulder with her husband, carving out a life for themselves and their children from the still-untamed wilderness in the new state of Idaho. "Demeaning" is not at all the word for the life she lived, and you *know* that women like her were women who commanded the respect of their husbands, their sons, and all the men who knew them. But a woman in the 50s who was just supposed to stay at home and keep her hair nice and play bridge and put the TV dinner in the oven at the right time and remember to be charming when her husband rolled in the door from doing big important stuff out in the world—"demeaning" is just about right.

I fully realize that I am painting with hugely broad strokes here. There are a million other factors which had to have contributed to the situation, some beginning back in the Enlightenment of the eighteenth century, others going all the way back to the Garden of Eden. And I have only barely waved at the obvious factor that was World War II, the return of the GIs, and the psychological effects the war had on both the men and the women. I cheerfully grant all that. Those were all important ingredients, but I would argue that the prosperity of the 50s and the subsequent ease of living was a direct cause of the purposelessness that all the women appeared to be feeling. This also explains why Friedan proposed the solution that she did. Women were unhappy from being underchallenged, so it makes sense that she thought the problem would be solved by the more challenging work which was available outside the home.

She thought that if the women could be offered something bigger to tackle, then they would find the fulfillment they sought. I follow the logic. In fact, I'm genuinely sympathetic to the whole situation.

7.

EXCUSING BOREDOM

B ut just because I understand and sympathize with the women who felt bored and underchallenged doesn't mean I think it was excusable. Let's say a man who is genuinely talented really throws himself into his work and subsequently makes a crazy killing in his business at age twenty-three. He decides to quit while he's ahead and retires with a fat bank account, and then proceeds to spend his days playing video games. I can understand how he could be initially thrilled, but that it would all get really old really fast, and he would soon feel super bored and underchallenged. On the other hand, that's no one's fault but his own. I'm not suggesting that the women were blameless, or that it was inevitable that the story would go the way it did. I'm certainly not suggesting it was the fault of the technology or the mass-produced goods or the capitalism or the general prosperity of the country. To whom much is given, much is required. Women had just been handed a crazy blessing—something far, far beyond what any women had ever been given in any century, in any culture in the world. But instead of deep gratitude, they began complaining. Instead of using those blessings to raise the bar and achieve more than any women had been able to achieve before them, they started fussing—basically doing their own little reenactment of the Israelites in the wilderness.

When you read that story, don't you always wonder how the Israelites were able to be so petty and self absorbed? They were having manna fall out of heaven on them every day. Manna. I mean seriously—bread out of heaven? Who gets that? No one gets that! How many people have starved in wildernesses since the dawn of time, and no manna ever dropped on them? And yet the Israelites were spared. They were given something spectacular, unprecedented, and completely miraculous. But how long did it take them to get fussy? "Who shall give us flesh to eat? We remember the fish, which we did eat in Egypt freely; the cucumbers, and the melons, and the leeks, and the onions, and the garlic: But now our soul is dried away: there is nothing at all, beside this manna, before our eyes." They were given something staggeringly amazing, and they got bored about it. Bored and fussy.

We tend to think of boredom and fussiness as small scale, little offenses that sometimes just happen to us like head colds. Sometimes we get in a mood. Sometimes we get bored and tired of everything and start feeling sorry for ourselves. Sometimes we feel a bit complainy. When we get into that mood, we want people to affirm us and support us, and when someone else gets that way, we think that we should put our arm around them and listen to their hard time and sympathize. But in the story of the Israelites, the boredom wasn't a small deal. They wanted meat, and so God dropped sick amounts of meat on them. Truly sick amounts. Quails flew in from the sea and then fell down and died all around the camp. Dead quails were piled waist-high for ten miles in every direction. God dropped the meat they demanded, saying they would eat it until it came out their nostrils, and then He struck them with a great plague while the meat was still between their teeth, and the people died. Getting bored and fussy about God's blessings is not a small deal, and sometimes when we demand more from God, He gives it to us and we choke on it.

The bored women of America in the 60s demanded more. "The Egyptians get to eat cucumbers and we don't and that's unfair and our souls are being sucked out! The men get to climb the corporate ladder and we don't and that's unfair and our souls are being sucked out! We demand the right to eat meat! We demand the right to leave our children behind!" God gave the Israelites what they asked, but it wasn't a blessing to them—they died with it still in their mouth. The *actual* blessing that God had given them was the very thing they were bored of and had walked away from, and in the 60s, the prosperity that God had showered on the women was the blessing they got bored of and walked away from. The women of our country demanded meat, and God has given it to us not, I think, as a blessing, but rather as a curse.

A loud and demanding fussiness has actually been one of the defining features of the feminist movement from the very beginning, and (although I'm sure they would prefer the word *angry* to *fussy*) the feminists themselves would not only recognize themselves in that description, they would be proud to own it. The first-wave feminists were known for their militant protests, and in fact the word *suffragette* was apparently first coined because of some of their political tactics such as hunger strikes, which they had learned from the Russians,[1] and which resulted in the women being force-fed in prisons. (The jolly Mrs. Banks from *Mary Poppins*, dancing around and singing "Sister Suffragettes," is not, perhaps, the most reliable historical picture.) The second-wave feminists self-consciously embraced the angry thing, and "demanding" their rights is one of their trademark moves, the louder the better. "I am woman, hear me roar" and all that. In itself, this should be enough to cause thinking Christian women concern. Whenever someone begins issuing demands to the universe about what is owed to them, we ought to be dubious. This is fundamentally at odds with biblical teaching on what is an obedient (and effective) response to injustice. Christ did not tell us that when someone takes our coat we should

1. Kevin Grant, "British Suffragettes and the Russian Method of Hunger Strike," *Comparative Studies in Society and History* 53.1 (January 2011), 113-143.

loudly demand its immediate return. He did not urge us to throw elbows when someone tries to sit in the most important seat. When we are reviled, He did not tell us to make sandwich boards and picket. When we are struck, we are not told to strike back harder. When Paul was wrongly imprisoned, he didn't commence organizing a prison riot or, for that matter, go on a hunger strike. And yet, aggressively demanding that everyone give women what is owed to us has been the entire campaign strategy of the feminist movement from Day One.

Note that I am not maintaining that the problem which provoked the feminist response was negligible in some way. I truly believe that the cultural expectations for women were extremely problematic in the 50s. But dealing with that obediently would have looked very, very different than the tightly wound yelling of the feminists. The women in the 50s were not being actively oppressed like, for instance, women in Muslim cultures often are. They were, however, suffering under the soft oppression of not being thought capable of anything very impressive, challenging, or important. Housewives of the 50s were expected to keep the house tidy, keep the children tidy, keep themselves tidy—and that pretty well covered it. Friedan quoted a 1960 *New York Times* article to that effect: "In the last year, the problem of the educated housewife has provided the meat of dozens of speeches made by troubled presidents of women's colleges who maintain, in the face of complaints, that sixteen years of academic training is realistic preparation for wifehood and motherhood."[2] The 1950s picture of an ideal housewife was one in which a woman's intellect played no significant role. That truly is a suffocating position to be in, but if the women had wanted to change that, they could have done it by actually deciding to accomplish impressive, challenging, and important things. There was plenty enough freedom for that, if they had wanted to go that route. Had they taken what they had been given and turned a huge profit on it, the conclusion would have been obvious to everyone. They could have *earned* the respect they craved, but instead of that, they began to loudly *demand* it.

One of the reasons that feminists took the route they did (that of demanding respect rather than deciding to earn it) was that they believed, along with Friedan, that the home simply did not offer the scope for anything. What was there to do in the home besides change diapers and dust? They had already done all that, and there was nothing in the domestic sphere that could give them dignity, purpose, and the fulfillment they coveted. If they were going to do something to earn respect, it would have to be "out there," somewhere. And if they were going to do it "out there" then they would have to yell and march and chant and bang on the inside of their front door until someone let them out into the corporate world where they could compete with the men and prove their worth.

The women of the 50s genuinely needed to be liberated, that much is indisputable. The feminists believed that what

---

2. Friedan, *The Feminine Mystique*, 50-1. The *New York Times* article was published June 28, 1960.

women needed liberation *from* was their domesticity and motherhood, but after much diligent work in that direction, it appears to be a dead end. Women are still unhappy, and Friedan's proposed solution has turned out to be a dud. Women need liberating now more than ever.

Friedan was the fan which blew the dwindling embers of feminism back into the roaring flame that we know as second-wave feminism, but she certainly was not the only player in the movement. Among others, one popularly known radical feminist was Gloria Steinem, founder of *Ms.* magazine and outspoken supporter of abortion. She herself had an abortion in London in 1956, and in 1969 she attended an abortion speak-out in a New York church basement—she credits that as being the moment she became an active feminist. In fact, much of her agenda was to take the idea of an abortion speak-out, drag it out of the basement into the light of day, and slap it down in the public square where everyone had to confront it. In the very first issue of *Ms.* magazine, which appeared in 1972, they featured a petition called "We had Abortions" that was signed by fifty-three well-known women even though abortion was still illegal. Her campaign has always been to remove the stigma attached to abortion, and she was famous for saying things like, "If men could get pregnant, abortion would be a sacrament."[3] In 1973, a year after the founding of *Ms.*, the Supreme Court issued its decision on *Roe v. Wade*. Abortion became legal in the

---

3. Steinem didn't coin that phrase, but she did make it famous. She credits an old woman taxi driver for saying it first.

United States, and another point went up on the board for the feminists. Even though abortion has been legal for the last forty years in America and has become extremely common, Steinem is still working to make it even more normal. In 2006, *Ms.* reissued its "We had Abortions" petition and asked all its readers to sign. Steinem doesn't just want abortion to be legal, she wants it to be normal and accepted and wholesome.

I find it interesting to look at the dates and timelines of these notable feminists. Back in Jane Austen's day we had Mary Wollstonecraft, and she died young after giving birth to her daughter, Mary Shelley. When Mary Shelley was twenty-three, Susan B. Anthony was born. In fact, their lives overlapped by thirty-one years. When Anthony was fifty-nine, Margaret Sanger was born, and their lives overlapped by twenty-seven years. When Sanger was fifty-five, Gloria Steinem was born—their lives overlapped by thirty-two years—and Steinem is alive today. Susan B. Anthony was born in 1820, very nearly two hundred years ago, and in one sense that's a very long time. On the other hand, by the time she died, Margaret Sanger was already well into her activism. And by the time Sanger died, Steinem was already in her thirties. Steinem is still a force to be reckoned with today. Three American women who could easily have known one another, who, through sustained and focused effort, managed to completely upend this nation. Three women, three constitutional amendments, and one Supreme Court case, each of which completely changed the face of the country. Emancipation, Prohibition, Suffrage, Abortion—none of these were insignificant changes.

But what on earth do those issues have in common? As we look back at some of the things that feminists have fought for, some of them seem like a positive good . . . but if they were fighting for good things—and winning—what on earth has gone wrong with our country, and why are we in this mess? We're now in the middle of third-wave feminism (at least by most accounts), and as far as I can make out no one really knows what that is for sure. There are a lot of angry women wishing they could be crusaders but lacking a clear cause to fight for, since all the major objectives have been accomplished. It's generally just a lot of muddle and lack of momentum, with feminists running in circles and bumping into each other and jumping on board with issues like the fight for transgendered bathrooms and getting confused about what the difference is between feminism and gay rights. But despite the fact that they don't seem to know what they're doing, they are still causing a lot of damage to what's left of our nation's morals. Whereas the second-wave feminists were opposed to things like pornography and prostitution because of the obvious fact that they exploit women, the third-wave feminists are more likely to approve of those things. How do we sort all this out? How on earth can we connect the dots between "Slavery should be illegal," "Women should be allowed to vote," "Alcohol should be illegal," "Birth control should be legal," "Abortion should be legal," and "I should get to go into any bathroom I want and identify as any gender I feel like"? Some of that list seems good, some seems wicked, some seems completely beside the point. And yet, for whatever reason, these causes are historically linked, and the fact that oftentimes the feminists were fighting against legitimate evils makes Christians get all confused and wonder if we should be feminists after all.

However, this is one of these instances in which it is vitally important to think like an adult and not a child. Picture one of those backseat arguments where the boy says, "All girls are stupid," and the rejoinder from the sister fires back, "Nuh-uh! *No* girls are stupid! Mom! Tell him that no girls are stupid!" The fact that they are contradicting each other does not mean that they are having an intelligent argument. As we think through this issue, it's important that we be able to get beyond that level of interaction and analysis.

So let's glance back through the issues that leading feminists fought for.

1. Mary Wollstonecraft objected to the argument made by Rousseau that women ought not to be educated. As do I.

2. Susan B. Anthony thought that slavery is a social evil. As do I.

3. Susan B. Anthony thought that drunk husbands and fathers are a social evil. As do I.

4. Susan B. Anthony thought that women should have the rights of citizens. As do I.

5. Margaret Sanger thought women dying of back-alley abortions was a social evil. As do I.

6. Betty Friedan thought the superficiality of the ideal housewife in the 50s was a social evil. As do I.

7. Gloria Steinem thinks pornography is a social evil. As do I.

Will I call myself a feminist then? Not for the wide world.

And here's why. It's important to identify *what* to fight against—but it's equally important to know *why* to fight and *how* to fight. Let me illustrate with the issue of abortion. I am opposed to abortion, and I think it should be illegal. Does that mean I agree with everyone else who is opposed to abortion? Absolutely not. For instance, I would be opposed to a man who wanted to bomb abortion clinics and assassinate abortion doctors. We may be agreed on *what* to fight against—but we are on opposite sides when it comes to the question of *how* to fight. And the issue of *how* is important enough that I would never want to identify myself with that man. In this case, *how* trumps *what*. If we bombed every abortion clinic in the nation and effectively eliminated all abortions in that way, we would still be a country of murderers. This is why superficial agreement on various issues can be so damaging in the long run—the superficial agreement is masking the fact that there is *actually no agreement* at all.

The *why* question can be equally important because it reveals the underlying assumptions—and those assumptions are always motivating forces for other issues and not just the one currently under discussion. So do I agree with Wollstonecraft that women should be educated? Absolutely. But I'm fundamentally opposed to her when it comes to the question of *why*. The way she would answer that question would also reveal *why* she was a socialist, *why* she believed in free love, *why* she supported the French Revolution—and meanwhile, the way I would answer the question of *why* would reveal that I'm a Christian.

The *how* and the *why* questions are important because they reveal the *trajectory* of the idea, whereas the *what* question is static. If you were going on a trip and needed to take a plane to get there, you would not go to the airport, ask yourself, "What is that? Is that a plane?" and if the answer was yes, climb on. *Where* the plane is headed matters. If you climb onto the wrong plane, the fact that you got the *what* question right will actually work against you. Because you got that question right but didn't think about the direction the plane was headed is why you're now stranded in Iceland. If you had actually gotten the *what* wrong and climbed onto a luggage cart instead of a plane, the consequences would have been much less dramatic.

Trajectory matters, and the trajectory of the feminist movement has been opposed to Christianity since day one. We need to get over the fact that sometimes we happen to agree with feminists on this or that issue. Just because we occasionally agree with the *what* does not mean we were ever agreed on the *how* or the *why*. And those are deeply important questions because they often reveal something we would whole-heartedly oppose on every level. It's not enough to look back at people like Susan B. Anthony, ask *what* she was fighting for, and then sign on with her causes and assume she was a hero. The *how* and the *why* matter, and from the very beginning the feminists have answered those questions differently than any Christian should. Out of the feminist leaders whom we have looked at, each and every one of them was not just a generic unbeliever who had never thought about religion one way or another— each one was philosophically *opposed* to Christianity, and that is not an irrelevant detail. These were all intelligent women, and they understood the implications of their positions. They had thought these things through. And the Christians who have been duped by it, Christians who have thought about these questions in an embarrassingly superficial manner, are the reason we are in the current demolition derby that is our country right now. The feminist cause has been advanced for the last two centuries in large part through the diligent efforts of sincere but muddle-headed Christians who never bothered to ask *how* and *why*, and jumped on board anyway—and now they're confused by all the consequences they never saw coming. They've been diligently playing basketball and never noticed that they were shooting on the wrong hoop—they still can't figure out why the scoreboard doesn't look better.

If we want to salvage anything from this wreck, we need to go back to the beginning and ask some very basic questions, and take care to think about them like adults. We need to drop some of our preconceived ideas and some of our cultural baggage, and try to analyze these questions like intelligent Christian women, women who are willing to honestly question some things that we may have always just taken for granted.

WHAT ARE WOMEN DESIGNED FOR?

T hat is the question, isn't it? What are we made for? What's our role? Surely that's the most basic of questions. What did God make us to do? Are we cutting *with* or *against* the grain in our daily pursuits?

We all know how frustrating it is to be using the wrong tool for a job. When my husband was getting his doctorate, we moved across the ocean to Oxford, England, with five small children and only what we could fit into our suitcases. Needless to say, there were a few gaps in our household as we settled into our new home. For instance, a can opener. I had packed one kitchen knife with me, and felt pretty smug to have been that prepared, but I hadn't thought to bring a can opener. And then when I grocery shopped for the first time, I forgot that important detail and came home with a bunch of tuna for the children's lunch that day, due to the sad shortage of peanut butter in English grocery stores. You can imagine the scene: Me, hacking away at a tuna can with a steak knife, making an absolute mess, little to no headway on the actual problem, and generally imperiling the lives of everyone within a five-foot radius. And of course, once I had pried the lid off the can enough to coax the tuna out of the opening, I had to do it again repeatedly because five hungry children require much more than one measly can. The tool worked in the end, but barely. That's not at all what it was designed for or what it's good at. I would have been equally up against it if I had been trying to slice tomatoes with a can opener. Design matters. The intent of the designer matters. And we women, as God's creatures, are *designed* by him to fulfill a particular role. How many women are out there living frustrated, impossible lives because they're trying to be a can opener when God actually made them a knife?

So what are we designed to be? What are the problems for which we are the solutions? To even ask that question is to part company with the trend of current thought and historic feminism, because of course in a godless universe we weren't *designed* for anything. In an evolutionary world we would eventually be able to accommodate ourselves to whatever situation we find ourselves in. Maybe eventually womankind would grow feathers, maybe we would grow careers. We would adapt. Change. Become. We could be anything we want to be, as untold numbers of Disney movies, pop songs, TV commercials, and Oprah have told us for decades. In an evolutionary world that might be true, but then again, we don't live in that world. We live in a world God designed, on purpose, and He had certain things in mind as He did so. We aren't all exactly alike, no. And we can grow, mature, and change, sure. But we can't grow past the fixed limits that He has built into our natures. Just as animal breeders know, you can alter a species only so much until you bump into a ceiling, past which it cannot change. You can't make chickens get indefinitely bigger. Sooner or later they're as big as they're going to be, as if there is some internal and fixed limit to how much variation the species can handle. The same is true of plants. You can make tomatoes a little bit bigger, yes, but you can't make them the size of Volkswagens. At some point, the expertise of the breeder no longer matters and the project just stops working.

And if God designed women for a specific purpose, if there are fixed limits on the feminine nature, then surely it would follow that when we are living in accordance with those limits and purpose we will be in our sweet spot. That's where we'll shine. Where we'll excel. And where we will find the most fulfillment.

If your hackles are already going up at that, then it's probably because you're afraid that in the end, what God designed you for is unexciting, unfulfilling, demeaning, and generally dull. You're already picturing the sadly colored suburban house, the minivan, and the long boring afternoons with a flavorless casserole to look forward to. But just stop and think for a second. What do we know about

God? Is He interested in creatures that are dull, underappreciated, and underutilized? Oh for pity's sakes. He's the God who created the tiger. The eagle. The sun. The palm tree. Why on earth, when He got to mankind, would He suddenly decide that He wanted to top it all off with a creature that's not allowed to live up to its full potential and has to sputter along at 10 percent output, never allowed to get out of first gear? I think we're safe on that front. I'm pretty sure that we'll find that what God has created us for is far more breathtaking, crazy, scary, and glorious than we have wanted to assume, and I don't think any of us, if we throw ourselves into the roles that He sets for us, will find ourselves bored. So remove from your mind all stereotypes of mid-century housewives, of china-doll femininity, of Victorian ladies swooning, of women not allowed to think for themselves or talk to the men about anything interesting or important. Set all that aside, whether those are things that make you gag or things you think look pretty fun. Drop all that, and let's just work through the question of what God made women *for*.

8.

SUBDUE

The first and most obvious thing God made us to do is *work*. Hard. In the Garden of Eden, before there was sin, before there was death, before there were tears, there was work. Work is not actually an enemy or a result of the fall—it was part of the "good" world God had made. When God first created Adam, he gave him a task. Not only that, it was a bigger task than any other human has been given. The first man was given a wild and empty planet, and he was told to *subdue* it (Gen. 1:28). This was a very tall order, obviously, and it was a job that was too big for Adam to handle alone—so much so that, as a creature with a role to play, he was insufficient. In fact, everything that God had created up until Adam was declared "good." God created light and it was good. He created the sun and moon and they were good. He created the sea and the land and they were good. He created the trees and the plants and they were good. He created the animals and they were good. He created a man, and suddenly . . . it was not good. It was *not good* that man should be alone—he needed a helper. And we already know what he needed the help for—he had been given the job of taming an entire planet. So the first thing we should note about the creation of Eve is that she was created specifically to assist Adam in his work, because he was insufficient for the task of conquering a world alone. When God created the first and perfect woman, He made a *worker* meant to stand by Adam's side as the two of them, together, took dominion of the earth.

When the 60s feminists were chomping at the bit to get out there and work, they were doing so because that's what God made us for. God didn't look at Adam in the garden and say, "It is not good for man to be alone, he needs something pretty to look at." The 50s idealized notion of a woman who only exists to look pretty and make the house look pretty is just as much a revolt against the creation order as the radical feminist agenda is—it's just a revolt against a different part. The Victorian ideal of a tender, swooning, delicate woman who is incapable of getting her lily white hands dirty is a *rebellious* ideal, forgetting what it was Eve was created for.

God did not create women to lounge around in picturesque poses, occasionally embroidering a handkerchief. It's interesting to me that historically, the moments when western culture's prosperity has turned women into merely decorative objects are the moments that ended up being preludes to feminism. The Victorian feminine ideal, that of the beautiful but helpless china doll, came right on the heels of the giant leap in standard of living that was the result of the Industrial Revolution. The story that played out in the 50s and 60s was actually a story that we had seen before. The Industrial Revolution in America had produced a huge improvement in quality of life, and the feminine ideal ended up being reduced to that of the merely ornamental.

However, as we've seen, that lasted only so long, and then the women revolted and we saw the birth of the suffragettes, the flappers, the "modern woman." After World War II and the subsequent age of ease and prosperity, women were once again subsiding into the merely decorative, and we were then treated to the 60s. I believe this is because you cannot successfully take real, true, hard work away from women. It goes directly against our design, and sooner or later the whole thing will backfire. Imagine if you were to take a racehorse and try to treat it like it was one of your childhood My Little Ponies. You wanted it to stay in your backyard all day, looking beautiful, munching the grass, and generally just being mellow while you braided its mane and tied sparkly bows in its tail. Sooner or later reality will manifest itself. A racehorse cannot be cooped up like that. Even animals get genuinely depressed under such circumstances, and how they will deal with that depression is a bit of a roll of the dice. Perhaps the horse will turn aggressive, perhaps it will run away, perhaps it will kick down your rose trellis and bite people. But none of this should be a shock. You cannot treat a racehorse like a doll and hope for the best. You cannot use a knife as a can opener and expect awesome results.

And women were created by God to run. To charge at things. To work like crazy. I think this is actually why women *can* be incredibly successful in the corporate world—because, contrary to the beliefs of traditionalists who think that "weaker vessel" means that women are too tender to do anything much, women are actually capable of killing themselves for others. If a woman successfully replaces a family with a career in her personal priorities, she is capable of laying herself down for it to an almost absurd degree. That won't necessarily make her happy, mind you. If the racehorse figures out how to run in a circle in the backyard over and over and over all day, it's showing you that it's capable of running—but surely everyone can see that the setting is all wrong. The horse is blowing off steam, not truly doing what it loves and what it was made to do. It's actually capable of so, so much more if it were given the scope. Women can throw themselves at the corporate world, and they can do it for the long haul. But the setting is wrong. It's like the horse running in a small circle again and again and again. Women would be capable of so, so much more if they were given the scope.

I know this is a completely foreign concept. We've been told that the corporate world is the place where there is scope. The career world is the wide open field where we can run—it's the domestic world that coops us up. We've been conditioned to see it this way. But the reverse is actually true. Ironically, there's a whole world, wide open and waiting for us, a world where we could truly run—but the feminists don't know where it is. Despite the fact that they have been waging a very noisy campaign for freedom, they have actually just led us into a very boring dead end.

9.

FILL

The other part of the creation mandate given to Adam in Genesis was that he needed to *fill* the earth with the human race (Gen. 1:28 again), and obviously this is not something he could do on his own, since a lone man is completely helpless on this front. Adam could have tried all his life long and not produced a single new human, so a helper for this part of the task was clearly necessary. Woman was the solution to this problem.

However, it is important to note that Eve was provided to Adam as a helper in *both* of his tasks—in both subduing the earth and in filling it—she was not required for the job of filling alone. Eve was not given to Adam simply because by himself he couldn't have babies. She was there to help with the enormous task of taming the planet, and another *man* wouldn't have been the right answer. Women are not here simply as the necessary apparatus by which more men are introduced into the world. If God had wanted a race of all males, He could have made one. He made women because women are necessary to the *entire* mission, not simply because God couldn't think of another way to get more men into the world to do all the real work.

However, that said, let's not forget to notice that filling the earth *was* actually part of the job given to Adam. It is true that cultures in the past and some traditionalists now are tempted to revolt against women being involved in the "subdue" part of the creation mandate. But overwhelmingly, that's not the problem of our generation. American women have been in full-scale rebellion against the "fill" part of the creation mandate ever since the First Wave of feminism. Elizabeth Cady Stanton, well before the Civil War, was arguing that a woman should have control over her childbearing. She referred to this as "voluntary motherhood." Margaret Sanger extended that principle to birth control and abortion. Betty Friedan wanted us to throw off our bondage to our "merely biological" role, and that has been the agenda of the feminist movement for the entirety of the twentieth century. The desire for sexual freedom without the attendant results and the demand for birth control and abortion to be treated as basic human rights— this is rebellion against one of the fundamental jobs which Eve was created to do.

On a physical level, women are designed to have babies, and this is so terribly obvious it's almost embarrassing. Everything about us is meant for mothering, from being sexually attractive to men in the first place, to being able to conceive, to the ability to weave together another little human inside of us without even trying, to the breasts that feed the baby, to all the mothering instincts that are hard-wired into us. We live with the reality of our fertility monthly. This is not a minor part of our design, it *is* our design. And the feminist agenda has been systematically attempting to separate women from their creational purpose in this regard for the last century and more.

The desire to get out into the workplace was never the whole package—and the fact that feminists talk about sex all the time is no accident. What is the biggest hindrance to a career? Being tied down by children. And unless women are willing to sacrifice their sexuality in the pursuit of their career and become nuns in devout service to the corporation, they have to deal with the fact that they will get pregnant. And thus it is that the feminist movement has been all about separating sex from motherhood from the very beginning. The battle is now so completely won that even many married Christians couples think of birth control almost as a sacrament, and many treat the idea of babies as an optional add-on to their relationship. We live in a society which despises fruitfulness, tolerating it only when it is a sort of self-conscious decision—a baby added on as a little garnish on top of a successful career like the small flourish of kale on the side of your dinner plate. Not really necessary, just decorative, and definitely not the point of the meal.

Eve was created in order to help Adam with both tasks—filling and subduing the earth. But somewhere along the line we've gotten ourselves tangled up and have started to see those two tasks as if they were an either–or situation. You can either subdue or you can fill. You can either "work" or you can have babies. Different generations in recent memory have leaned towards one or the other of these, and so the teeter-totter has wobbled back and forth on what is considered culturally acceptable for women to do. But the truth is that women were created for *both*. God made Eve to be innately gifted for and driven to do both of those things. If you try to make women, as a group, do nothing difficult except have babies, they'll be wretchedly unhappy. If you try to make women, as a group, work like dogs but deny their roles as mothers, they'll be wretchedly unhappy.

IO.

HELP

I'm afraid it's quite obvious in the creation account of Genesis that Eve was created to help Adam, not the other way around. The apostle Paul also makes this point abundantly clear in that terribly unpopular passage in 1 Corinthians 11, "Neither was the man created for the woman; but the woman for the man" (v. 9). And this, just as much as the insinuation that we women were created to be mothers, smacks straight into all of our culturally acceptable, politically correct categories. Even conservative women can resent Eve being relegated to the status of a mere "helper," and it bugs us that Paul would be so insensitive as to harp on that point. It seems so typically male, and so offensively oblivious to the fact that we are capable individuals with gifts and talents and abilities that are *in no way inferior* to the men's gifts and talents and abilities. Being classified as "helpers" feels just so demeaning.

I'm also afraid, however, that the Scriptures are just pretty straightforward on this point. Eve was created to help, not to be the commander in chief. Adam was not brought into the picture to be her sidekick, and she was not brought into the picture to live an independent life, fulfilling her own dreams while Adam did his thing separately. It does us no good at all to try to take the plain meaning of Scripture and turn it inside out and then stand it on its head, as many "Christian" feminists have spent their time attempting to do. (As a side note, it's ironic to me that so often, women try to prove that they should be allowed to be pastors and elders—and their proof for this is that they demonstrate to everyone that they are completely incapable of reading the text. Not exactly their best foot forward if they want to be taken seriously as biblical scholars.)

However, there's always more than one way to misinterpret a text. Feminists deal with the scriptural teaching here by trying to explain it away and pretend it didn't happen, but others have *embraced* what they assumed Paul was teaching in a way that was equally problematic.

The real trouble comes in when we read "helper" and mentally say, "inferior." Once you've done that you're on the wrong path completely. One sees how it happens, of course. "Helper" implies that someone *else* is in charge, and the helper is in a secondary role. And having one person chosen to be the "head" (1 Cor. 11:3) makes us assume that those responsible for placing that person in charge must think that person is inherently better at certain things—that must be why they were chosen for the task. And if they are "better" at certain things that implies that the one who wasn't chosen is "worse." And "worse" obviously implies "inferior." We run through those steps so quickly we don't even see ourselves doing it—we say "helper" and think "inferior" without even noticing the intervening steps.

Some people read the Bible this way and then either get mad or try to explain it away (feminists), and others do it and say "amen" to what is actually their own misconception (chauvinists), but oddly, they're both making the same mistake. They're missing the meaning of the text in exactly the same way—they just react to it differently on an emotional level. But we should make sure to notice that both of them are in the same camp when it comes to how they interpret the text. And that interpretation is fundamentally mistaken. In 1 Corinthians 11, Paul is clearly pointing out differences between men and women and our creational roles, and for us moderns, that in itself is enough to make us immediately ask whose side Paul is on. "Is he on the side of the men or the women?" To even acknowledge that two things are distinct or different from each other makes us instinctively try to give them a score as if they're competing with one another. We do this so swiftly that we don't even notice that *we're* the ones importing that suggestion into the passage. It would truly be impossible to make this point and *not* quote Chesterton here:

If I set the sun beside the moon,

And if I set the land beside the sea,

And if I set the flower beside the fruit

And if I set the town beside the country

And if I set the man beside the woman

I suppose some fool would talk

About one being better.[1]

Making the observation that one thing is fundamentally different from another is most emphatically *not* the same thing as insinuating that one is better than the other. For all of our culture's blathering on about "diversity," we actually aren't very good at dealing with it. We much prefer everything to be exactly the same, because it's so much simpler that way and doesn't make our heads hurt. Feminism resents the mere suggestion that women have a different role than men. And when God presents Eve to Adam as the corresponding puzzle piece that makes him complete, we are capable of turning that into an insult to all women everywhere—an insult that we either deeply resent if we're sympathetic with the feminists, or an insult that we use to hurl at the women if we're little chauvinist piggies.

---

1. G.K. Chesterton, originally unpublished but reprinted in Maisie Ward, *Gilbert Keith Chesterton* (New York: Sheed & Ward, 1943), 61.

II.

GLORIFY

S o what does that seemingly insulting and awfully problematic passage in 1 Corinthians 11 actually teach? Let's just walk through verses 3–12.

3 But I would have you know, that the head of every man is Christ; and the head of the woman is the man; and the head of Christ is God. 4 Every man praying or prophesying, having his head covered, dishonoureth his head. 5 But every woman that prayeth or prophesieth with her head uncovered dishonoureth her head: for that is even all one as if she were shaven. 6 For if the woman be not covered, let her also be shorn: but if it be a shame for a woman to be shorn or shaven, let her be covered. 7 For a man indeed ought not to cover his head, forasmuch as he is the image and glory of God: but the woman is the glory of the man. 8 For the man is not of the woman; but the woman of the man. 9 Neither was the man created for the woman; but the woman for the man. 10 For this cause ought the woman to have

power on her head because of the angels. [11] Nevertheless neither is the man without the woman, neither the woman without the man, in the Lord. [12] For as the woman is of the man, even so is the man also by the woman; but all things of God.

All the stuff about head coverings in this passage is actually terribly interesting and obviously important, but really a subject for another time.[1] Let's just focus on what Paul is telling us about our the relationship between the genders in the abstract.

First, he tells us that the head of woman is man, and the head of man is Christ, and the head of Christ is God. If you read that in a simplistic way, I agree that it can sound a bit offensive to women. I believe that's a pretty superficial reading of the verse (we'll get to that in a minute), but many Christian feminist scholars have devoted years of their lives and thousands of pages to doing extraordinary gymnastics with the grammar and the vocabulary of this verse. They will import scare quotes into the text as if Paul were using a funny voice when he said this—to show us we weren't really supposed to believe it.[2] Or they will turn themselves inside out trying to say the Greek word *kephale* ("head") doesn't really mean "head," which we would understand if we would only get dual master's degrees in Suspension of Disbelief and Corinthian Cultural Studies.

---

1. If you're still curious: Ben Merkle, "Head Coverings," *Credenda/Agenda* 12.3, p. 18 (http://www.credenda.org/archive/issues/12-3recipio.php).

2. Cf. Lucy Peppiatt, "Talking Heads 1," Theological Miscellany (Feb. 10, 2016), http://theologicalmisc.net/2016/02/talking-heads (accessed May 5, 2016).

Let me give you a somewhat morbid metaphor. Imagine a woman who is home alone and hears someone coming in at the front door. She panics, thinks it's a burglar come to plunder and raid and rape and pillage, so she grabs the shotgun, runs into the living room, and starts blazing away. In her panic, her aim is somewhat dubious, but because it's a shotgun she's successful in fatally wounding the man coming in. Unfortunately, it turns out it was her husband coming home from work and not actually a burglar. Now, in one sense she was fighting an unreal foe, because the burglar was a figment of her imagination, but there was a casualty nonetheless. I think the same thing is true of our breathless Christian feminists, flinging Greek grammatical and cultural trivia here and there and everywhere in an attempt to fight off the potential egregious offense to womanhood which is the apostle Paul. The problem is that he never was that, and if they could have just calmed down for a minute they could have seen it too. But calming down has never been their strong suit—they seem to have learned their research techniques from fainting goats.[3] In their haste to defend womanhood there *has* been a casualty—but the thing lying cold and dead on the floor is not patriarchy. What they've managed to kill is intelligent interaction with the plain meaning of the text.

But let's go back to verse 3 and look at it again. Paul is telling us that the head of woman is man and the head of

---

3. If you've never seen fainting goats, google them immediately. Really funny.

man is Christ and the head of Christ is God. After a superficial read, that can sound an awful lot like a totem pole of
importance, with women being at the tail end—the sorry
little caboose at the end of the train with everyone having
someone they get to boss around except for the women.
But it really *can't* mean that, can it? I mean, not unless we
want to fall into serious heresy. Because in that same line-
up, God is the head of Christ. If it sounds like women are
inferior to men in this passage, wouldn't that also imply
that Christ is inferior to God the Father? And that's an
interpretation that would fly in the face of all Trinitarian
orthodoxy and land us in the camp of the Arians. So unless
you're ready to become a Jehovah's Witness and deny Jesus'
deity, this verse can't *possibly* be about inherent superiority
and inferiority of men and women. And, in fact, Paul is
careful to clarify that he is not in fact arguing that. After
making the argument that woman was created for man,
he quickly adds on the clarification that in the Lord, men
and women are equals. "Neither is the man without the
woman, neither the woman without the man, in the Lord.
For as the woman is of the man, even so is the man also
by the woman; but all things of God." Paul doesn't want
anyone to go running away with the idea that the men are
the most important.

So if he isn't writing about inherent superiority, then
what *is* he saying? After he describes who is the head of
whom, Paul restates it another way. "For a man indeed
ought not to cover his head, forasmuch as he is the image

and glory of God: but the woman is the glory of the man. For the man is not of the woman; but the woman of the man" (vv. 7–8). This, again, sounds suspiciously like women are getting the short end of the deal here. God is glorious, of course, and then man is the image and glory of God, and then the woman is the glory of man. Once more we find the women at the bottom of the glory totem pole. The glory is sort of emanating out from the center, which is God, and getting progressively weaker the further it gets. So if men are like a shadow of God, then women are like a shadow of a shadow, the smallest ripple at the farthest edge. The super badly pixelated image. If we want to know what the glory of God is like we should look at the men because they're closer to it than the women are, right?

But to read it this way is to read it directly backwards. A quintessentially biblical and very Hebraic way of expressing a superlative is to use the form the *Song of Songs* or the *Holy of Holies*. We tend to read this Corinthians passage as if the glory is getting more and more diluted the further it gets away from the center. But stop and think in more biblical categories for a second. If Adam is the crown of creation, then Eve is the crown of the crown. Women are the glory of the glory. When you read of the Holy of Holies in Scripture, are you on the furthest fringe of the holiness, or are you closer to the center? Obviously the holiness isn't getting weaker as you go into the Holy of Holies, it's getting stronger, more distilled. Man was created as the image and glory of God, but then along came the woman—second—in an even more concentrated form. The glory of the glory of God. If men are the beer, women are the whiskey. The most potent, strong, and intoxicating version of the glory of God, not the weakest and most watered down. And ironically, this is exemplified by her being created second, as an equal but a helper, as an equal who willingly submits to her head.

In fact, that submission itself is what is so glorious, and that is because the willing submission of one equal to another—a submission offered out of love and not out of servitude—is a submission that pictures Christ. Christ, who, as Philippians 2:6 tells us, "being in the form of God, thought it not robbery to be equal with God: But made himself of no reputation, and took upon him the form of a servant, and was made in the likeness of men: And being found in fashion as a man, he humbled himself, and became obedient unto death, even the death of the cross" (Phil. 2:6–8). Christ was *equal* with God, but willingly humbled Himself. He offered Himself up in submission to God the Father, but *not because He was inferior.*

When a woman submits to her husband, her head, she is picturing that. She is picturing Christ, willingly submitting, as an equal, to *the* Head. But what is the end of the story when Christ submits to the Father, even to the point of death on the cross? "Wherefore God also hath highly exalted him, and given him a name which is above every name: That at the name of Jesus every knee should bow, of things in heaven, and things in earth, and things under the earth; And that every tongue should confess that Jesus Christ is Lord, to the glory of God the Father" (Phil. 2:9–11). That submission ends in exaltation. It ends in glory. He is lifted up and given the name that is above every name.

Of course God the Father and God the Son are equals. More than that, they are not just equals, they are one—but at the same time distinct from each other. In a similar way, of course Adam and Eve are equals. Eve *is* Adam after all—when he sees her he says, "this is bone of my bone, flesh of my flesh." She is him, separated from him, glorified, brought back to him to become one with him again. *Of course* they are equals.

Women need to stop being so offended about being asked to submit to an equal. Christ did not consider it robbery to humble himself and submit to an equal, and neither should we, because when we picture *that* submission we are picturing the most potent form of glory that there is. We are enacting the story that is at the very heart of all history, the most glorious story ever told. This is not a weak, watered down, pitiful little glory, the one the furthest away from the center. It is the most powerful, the most magnificent, the most intoxicating, the most concentrated picture of glory that can be found in creation. And we are privileged to be the ones asked to do it.

Because we women *are* the glory, it makes sense that we tend to be preoccupied with glori*fying*. We do this innately and without even having to think about it, in the same way that our bodies can create another human inside of us without us having to stop and read a manual about how to do it. God created us for this purpose, and we beautify and we glorify constantly. Sometimes we do this in obedient ways, sometimes in rebellious ways; sometimes we revolt against our innate desire to do this at all, but this is a deeply ingrained trait that God has built into womankind, and it just can't be completely smothered. We do it in small things like when we take an unholy looking bachelor pad and turn it into a beautiful home, or when we take a paycheck and turn it into a hot meal on the table that looks and smells and tastes amazing. Women are built to enflesh. To translate. Sometimes we do it without thinking, and sometimes we just can't help it. We can take the love of a man and woman and turn it into a fat little baby—a separate and distinct living picture of the oneness of his parents. We show our innate desire to beautify when we fix our hair, put on makeup, care about our clothes or our homes. We translate and enflesh when we take an abstract command like "hospitality" and turn it into a party with great music and good food. We embody, we enflesh, we multiply, and we transform cultures. Eve *is* fruitfulness.

But one thing we see again and again in both Scripture and in nature is that fruitfulness never comes by itself. There is never any spring unless there is first a winter. There is never any resurrection unless there has been a death. There is no flower growing that did not first begin as a seed that went into the ground and died, that cracked open, that broke, in order that life could come from it. There is no Easter unless there is first a Good Friday.

That is why submission is so essential to our role. Without submission there could be no true glory. Without death there could be no life from the dead. Without a seed going into the ground, no life could come up from that ground. When a woman submits, when she lays herself down, when she, like Christ, offers herself up to the death of humility, in submission to someone who is an equal, that is the field in which glory grows. In the words of Shelley, (although he meant it to be entirely godless), "If winter comes, can spring be far behind?" In Scripture, submission and glory *always* go together—and in that sequence.

And this is why, when women reject their duty of submission, the glory fades. This is why the cultural fruit of feminism is as intentionally ugly and barren as lesbianism. When submission leaves, the glory and the beauty and the fertility leave right along with it. If glory is a flame, submission is the oxygen that it needs in order to burn.

But not just any old submission. Abject servitude, the submission of a slave to a master, kills glory just as effectively as no submission at all. We see this with Islamic sharia law, we see this in ultraconservative, women-are-to-be-seen-and-not-heard-but-actually-not-really-seen-either sects, and oddly enough I think we also see it in our current freewheeling, sexually progressive culture that has supposedly shaken off all the tired old restrictions for women. It's interesting that our culture has attempted to amputate the fertility (the fruitfulness) of women, but keep the beauty of women, and the end result has been that women have become nothing more than sex objects. All that talk of liberation, and the result is that every woman's magazine is full of articles about how to please a man the same way a cheap hooker would. The way a slave would. Certainly not the way a free woman offers herself to an equal. Abject sexual servitude has become the standard for women in our culture, dominated by the paradigm of pornography, where a man can demand anything he wants and the woman must and will comply.

Not only have women allowed themselves to be manipulated into this, they have actively pursued it, thinking they are running away from the stringent requirements of submission. Most are too blind to even see what's happening to them. We have tried to cut our feminine glory in half, keeping the beauty but throwing away the fertility, and by perverting the glory in this way we have not removed the submission, but have rather made it demanding, monstrous, and hideous. Culturally, we have turned the norm of the sexual relationship between men and women into the relationship between a consumer and the product, the employer and the hired help, the master and the slave.

In our unbelieving, supposedly liberated culture, submission *is* demanded of women, but certainly not the submission of an equal to an equal. Running away from the scriptural requirement to submit to *one* man, as an *equal*, within the protection of marriage (because that's just too demeaning), has resulted in women living with the reality of abject submission to numerous men, with no protection at all, and with her bearing the entire weight of responsibility for the outcome. The fruit of this lifestyle must either be killed or she must raise the child alone.

It's worth noting, since conservatives have been known to miss this, that nowhere in Scripture are women, as a group, required to submit to men, as a group. Women are commanded to submit to their *own husbands* as to the Lord, nowhere are we required to submit to "men." Thank heavens. True submission, in true freedom, of one woman to one man, results in true glory and true fruitfulness. When we pervert or remove one part of this equation, the whole thing gets lost or twisted.

LIVING OUT OUR DESIGN

12.

HOME

If all of this is true, then how do we live in a way that maximizes our design? I've said that the feminist ideal of life in the corporate world (if that's what we're going to call the humdrum reality of the jobs most women do) is actually more like a racehorse stuck living its life in your backyard, and that recapturing a true understanding of femininity would be intense, challenging, scary, fulfilling, and culturally transformative. That's all good and well, but what does it actually look like? Where does a woman belong? Is she allowed to have a job? Is it true that a woman's place is in the home? These are some of those simple yes-or-no questions that actually can't be answered with a simple yes or no. There is much cultural baggage, both good and bad, that has surrounded this issue, and so some people want to dismiss the question as utterly ludicrous on the face of it, and others want to absolutize things in a simplistically wooden way. So let's just look at what the Scripture has to say about the whole thing.

Another obvious passage we need to reckon with is Titus 2. In this chapter Paul works his way through describing duties of old men, duties of young men, duties of old women, duties of young women, and duties of servants. We can assume from this that he is giving us a brief blueprint for the ideal Christian society. Paul essentially says, "When you have a group of Christians living as they ought, playing the roles God has created them for, here's what that will look like." What concerns us is the women—so let's just look at the verses addressed to them.

> [3] The aged women likewise, that they be in behaviour as becometh holiness, not false accusers, not given to much wine, teachers of good things; [4] That they may teach the young women to be sober, to love their husbands, to love their children, [5] To be discreet, chaste, keepers at home, good, obedient to their own husbands, that the word of God be not blasphemed. (Titus 2:3–5)

That can sound incredibly restrictive to many people—like Paul is describing a life of tedium, boredom, no talking, and general hideousness. But before we get too offended, think of what the opposite of Paul's list is, and see which one sounds more in keeping with faith and grace. Imagine a town (or a church) full of unholy, drunk old women who spend their time accusing people falsely and then in the off-moments teaching the young women to be unrestrained, to not love their husbands, to not love their children, to be undiscerning and immoral, to ignore their homes, to be bad, and to be disobedient to their husbands. Hmm. Not a tricky question. One sounds like faithfulness and the other sounds like a typical night on primetime TV. So rather than being offended at Paul here, let's go with him on this, submit ourselves to God's word, trusting that He has good things in store for us and not wretched things specially designed to make us waste all our gifts and abilities . . . and then let's try to really understand what He's saying here.

First off, let's look at the young women and their relationship to the home. In the King James Version that I quoted above, they are told to be "keepers at home." In other versions this is translated variously as "be busy at home," "working at home," "managers of their households." The women who are instructed to do this are young women who also apparently have husbands and children—basically, women who have households. If there *is* a household, the wife and mother of that household is the one who should be running it. If you think about it, a household grows up around a woman—without her, there would be no household in the first place—and if that is the position you find yourself in, then Paul is telling you what to do about it. Take care of it. Manage it. If you have a household, then you have been handed your talents by the Master, and He expects you to turn a profit on it. You're not allowed to take the talent He has given you, bury it in the ground, and go off to try and earn a profit in some other way that you find more interesting. Here's your job—nail it.

It's also interesting to note that at the end of this section Paul specifically connects this to the gospel mission—this is a witness to the outside world. When unbelievers see women like this, they will be unable to blaspheme the Word of God. This is what a city on a hill looks like. This teaching isn't meant to keep the women out of sight; it's describing the way that they can shine the light of the gospel on a lost and sinful culture. We have to trust God here, because oftentimes we want to be the ones to decide what will be a good witness. God says, "Here's how to be a good testimony," and we think He doesn't understand the nuances of modern society the way we do. A good testimony will *actually* turn out to look like something entirely different than what God said . . . and will look surprisingly like what we wanted to do anyway.

Ultimately, everything depends on the attitude with which we approach this command to be "keepers at home." Imagine asking your child to do a job. Let's say he's reading a book on the sofa, and you ask him to pick up the shoes he left in the middle of the floor and put them on the shelf. Let's envision various ways he might react. There's the straight-up disobedience route where he just flat ignores what you said. Or maybe he fusses, complains, argues, and instead of obeying, turns it into an hour-long drama at the end of which the shoes are still in the middle of the floor. Maybe he gives you a fat-face, looks at you with an "are you kidding me right now" expression, walks across to his shoes with that full-body floppy walk, picks up his shoes, hurls them at the shelf, and throws himself back on the couch in such a way as to let you know that you have completely ruined his afternoon.

Don't be that kid. When God tells you what to do, hop up and cheerfully do what He's asked of you. Embracing your role at home with a fussy heart, a fat-face, and a floppy walk is not the same thing as obeying. It certainly won't earn you a "well done, good and faithful servant." We should try to *please* our Master, not try to demonstrate how unreasonable we think He is.

So Titus 2 is fairly straightforward—women who are wives and mothers should be managing their households, and they should be doing so in such a way that they are gaining wisdom and experience to pass down to the younger women, and this will have an impact on the watching world. This also implies something worth noting: managing a household and being a godly wife and mother is a skill requiring practice, teaching, and expertise. There are two possible responses here. The first is where we assume that homemaking is a useless job, designed especially to keep women away from "real" work, so the fact that Paul thinks women need to instruct each other about how to get good at it just shows us what a low opinion he has of women. Or . . . and I would suggest this is the more faithful option . . . we assume that Paul is up to speed on the fact that God gave Eve to Adam as a necessary part of the creation mandate, and so when he tells us to keep the home, and we can't imagine what on earth there is to do there—this is *our* problem, not his. Maybe we need to expand our vision of what it means to keep the home. Rather than seeing Titus 2 as evidence of Paul's low view of women, perhaps we should see it as evidence of Paul's high view of the importance of the home.

The next question, of course, is whether keeping the home necessitates staying in it all the time. I would suggest that we are often far too simplistic about this. A household is bigger than the house itself, and as Paul describes the duties of a wife and mother, it is clear that her duties are defined by the people she is surrounded by and not simply her street address. What it looks like to keep a household running varies from century to century, from country to country, from family to family, and from season to season. A woman keeping a house full of small children looks different than a woman keeping a house full of teenagers, which in turn looks different from a woman keeping a house where the grandchildren come back to visit. Paul recognizes this in the Titus passage—he expects that an older woman has different duties than a young one. Clearly Paul acknowledges the seasons in a woman's life and is not wooden in prescribing what every female's daily to-do list should look like.

So could a woman be faithfully keeping her house, in exactly the way Paul tells her to, but also have "a job"? Well, the Proverbs 31 woman was doing it—so it would be ludicrous of us to say that women may not engage in any business ventures. *Of course* the Bible doesn't prohibit a woman making money. On the other hand, as I've written before, that's not really the problem of our generation. We've got bigger questions to answer. We are a generation that needs to recover a sense of the importance of the home, and the importance of wives and mothers who are *invested in their people.* In Proverbs 31, we can see from the way this woman's family responds to her that all of her work, all of her buying, selling, and trading, was a direct blessing to *them.* Her children rise up and call her blessed, the heart of her husband safely trusts her, he knows he will have no lack of gain. All of them are clothed in scarlet through this woman's diligent work—they aren't all at home fending for themselves while mom is off on another business trip or living her dreams in the corporate world. They didn't rise up in the city gates to say, "Well we are all really glad that she was able to fulfill herself and follow her dreams." The Proverbs 31 woman is an impressive, hard-working, high-achieving, high-earning woman—but it is all aimed at *her people.*

It's striking to me how our culture will talk about women who give up their careers to stay at home with their families. It's frequently framed in terms of a *betrayal of women*, which to me is an amazing thing to think about. The goal of feminism has been to make women feel a deep loyalty, a militant, ultrapatriotism to their "tribe"—and that tribe is womankind. The feminists tell us that our first duty is supposed to be to ourselves—and that is how we show solidarity with "women." After that, we can think about our husbands and kids—and if we don't do things in that order, we are letting down the rest of womankind. They want us to have a deep clan loyalty, but they want to redraw the lines of what our clans are. And the way the feminists want to draw tribal lines insists on splitting each and every family unit in half. *Of course* we should have a deep loyalty to our people—but our people are the husbands we promised to love until the grave takes us, and the little faces staring up at us, depending on us, loving us, needing us—not a nameless blob of humans who lack a Y chromosome and to whom we have never even been introduced.

Paul orients us toward what our focus should be and where our attention should stay, and that is on our households. I would never say that a wife's place is in the home, but I would absolutely say that a wife's *priority* should be her home. If a woman is managing her home in such a way that it fills up and overflows and spills out into business endeavors, it should be the kind of thing that is a blessing to her people—giving more to them and not less. Her home should be what she is pointed at, not the thing that she's trying to escape. As soon as a job (or anything else) begins to pull us away from our families, then we need to stop and reevaluate, remembering where God wants us to be focused. And at the same time, we must believe that keeping our priorities structured the way God has asked us to will be like being planted in the sunny and well-watered corner of the garden—it's not going to turn out to be a con.

That does affect how women should view their careers—and yes, it means that the way a woman relates to her outside jobs will be fundamentally different than the way a man relates to his. I would argue that we should be mature enough to understand and embrace that difference rather than being offended by it or feeling that it's unfair. We need to be the ones who are ready to own it, not resent it; ready to see that if we have a family, the work we do for that household is the most important work we could possibly be doing—and everything else needs to take a back seat.

Fundamentally, however, one of the most vital needs of our current day is to reorient how we think about the home itself. Women need to actually start using their imaginations and showing some innovation in this regard—and thankfully, imagination and innovation are two things that women, as a group, are particularly good at. We need to stop thinking of home as a triviality and begin seeing how deeply profound and fundamental it is. If we succeeded in doing this, the question of whether a woman needs to "remain in the house" would become a somewhat obsolete question. But if we want to see how we could move forward, we should first make sure we know where we're standing with regard to the past—so let's glance at that first.

Historically, in the pre–Industrial Revolution era, the home and the workplace were often (though certainly not always) linked. In medieval Europe or colonial America or first-century Israel, a man's trade was usually centered at his home, or he made his home at his place of business. In centuries past, if you wanted to commission a blacksmith, for instance, you would likely visit the man's home to conduct your business transaction (or he would visit yours), and then he would create your piece in his shop—which was also where he lived. A farmer obviously had his business very connected to his home. A winemaker lived where he worked. A butcher or baker likely sold his breads out of his shop and lived upstairs or in the back. Tavern keepers lived in the tavern. Clear exceptions to this would be soldiers, diplomats, builders, etc. And yet, for many households in this older economy, a wife and husband were both deeply involved in the "business" side of things, even if their particular emphases were different. But with the advent of the Industrial Revolution, the typical workplace moved away from the home and became centered elsewhere. In this new world, a man would leave his home in the morning and go to the factory or to the office to work rather than going to the shop out back. In the new economy, a wife could conceivably know little to nothing about her husband's trade, whereas in the older system it was likely that she was intimately acquainted with his business.[1] This more distinct separation of the spheres (combined with a

---

1. While coming to slightly different conclusions, I am indebted for this observation to Nancy Pearcey's section "Households at Work" in *Total Truth: Liberating Christianity from Its Cultural Captivity* (Wheaton, IL: Crossway, 2004) 327 ff.

substantial jump in standard of living) eventually led to a trivializing of the woman's traditional role, which had come to be seen as less difficult and less profound than the work being done "out there" by the husband. This of course was one of the contributing factors to women being seen (by themselves as well as by the men) as unequipped for and uninvolved in the actual important business of life. They started becoming merely decorative and ended by feeling "left behind," with all the interesting work now gone beyond their reach.

But think of it this way. The Industrial Revolution may have increased the distance between the world of the home and the world of business, but there is no doubt that this change did wonders for the world of business—which is what in turn led to the increased standard of living in the home. If you picture it like a bicycle, it's as if the Industrial Revolution pumped up one of the tires. We now live in a world with airplanes and iPhones and Netflix, and those are not things that can be manufactured in the shop out in the backyard. The old economy was simply not able to produce such things, and this world of convenience that we now enjoy is a direct result of an industrialized society which has figured out the benefits of division of labor. One of the bicycle tires—the business world—is pumped way up and is doing well, but because the back tire—the home—is woefully flat, the bike is still riding very rough. Our society may have iPhones, but it is rootless, disconnected, isolated, and unhappy. We have airplanes, which means that we can drift and wander more quickly and efficiently. We have Twitter and Snapchat, but no family tables and no loyalty. Much has been made of America's problem with obesity, and the culprit is usually assumed to be unhealthy convenience foods, consumerism, corn syrup, or something similar. But if you have ever looked at any kind of message board or "support group" for people struggling with their weight, one of the most outstandingly obvious features is that humans turn to food as a way of numbing deep unhappiness, loneliness, or betrayal. The fellowship *around* the food is what we deeply crave—and when that is absent, we often try to fill the void with more food. How much of America's obesity is not, as we assume, a problem with our food—but rather a problem with our dysfunctional homes? I don't think it's an accident that when mothers, *en masse*, threw off their aprons and walked out of the kitchen, our country, *en masse*, turned to convenience foods for both nourishment and solace, and now we have a national problem with obesity.

We desperately need to inflate that back tire, and that means the women need to think creatively. The Industrial Revolution massively expanded the possibilities in the world of business—the same could be done in the home if any of us bothered to give it a try. And in just the same way that innovation and progress in the business world directly impacted our standard of living in our homes, there is no doubt that the influence of strong homes on the business world would be equally profound.

We need to stop assuming there is a fixed limit to what can be done in the home—I'm convinced the boundaries are much farther out than any of us realize. The women who have chafed and left the home are basically saying that there is nothing that can be done about that back tire—it's hopeless—and they have gone to enjoy themselves at the front. Other conservative women have stayed in the back, insisting that flat tires are fine with them. Then there are those who want to dial back the clock and return to a pre–Industrial world in which father stays home, raising pigs and hoeing beets, trying to recapture an economy of four hundred years ago and living in some sort of separatist, self-sufficient, attempted utopia—arguing that we should let the air back out of the front tire again. But . . . here's a thought: what if we were to try pumping up the back one?

What if we were to try questioning our definition of homemaker? What if we were to use our imaginations and creativity? Too often we just accept the premise that a homemaker drives carpool, gets the casserole in the oven, and organizes the closets. Once those things are done, we feel like we have ticked all the boxes and now our time is our own. It's all too easy for us to *work* in order that we may have *leisure,* rather than working because we're convinced that we're building something phenomenal—and that mindset makes absolutely all the difference in the world. It is the difference between the employee and the boss, the hired help and the entrepreneur, the servant and the free man.

Imagine a woman who aims to get through all her housekeeping jobs as fast as possible so that she can enjoy her afternoons at the gym or on Facebook or whatever. That's a woman who will be looking for every corner she can possibly cut—from what kinds of recipes she picks to the kind of furniture she buys. She is acting like an *employee* fulfilling the duties that were prescribed by another—and as long as she tags the bases, no one can complain or ding her on her performance evaluation. Now imagine another woman who is *owning* her job as a housewife, who is convinced that it is culturally transformative work, and who sees the scope of her work as absolutely *vast*. Those are two women who are approaching nearly every task completely differently, and they will achieve very different things—in much the same way that two athletes can train right next to each other in the gym, but the one who is focused, diligent, and pushing himself will see drastically better results than the one who gets on the treadmill in body but not in spirit, and spends his time there catching up on TV shows.

Broadening our concept of what a woman's role actually *is* could also, I think, be hugely helpful to the large numbers of women who don't exactly fit into the quintessential "homemaker" mold. For example, what about single women? Or what about women with older children who now have more time on their hands? What about women who are more scientifically or mathematically gifted? If we define our roles too narrowly (which I think is most definitely the case) these are women who can feel displaced, left out, or unqualified in some way—*especially* if they are women who actually agree with everything I'm saying here. I can imagine a single woman, agreeing in principle that homemaking is culturally transformative work—and then concluding that she's on the outside looking in, or like she's sitting on the bench in the dugout while other women are out there actually playing. Now, it certainly *may* be true that she's sitting in the dugout—but it will only be true if that's where she has decided to sit.

Women are born translators. We take principles, abstract ideas, and then put flesh on them. This is just as much a single woman's gift as it is a married woman's—it's just that the application will look different. The single woman should look at the principles—and then figure out how to enflesh them in her particular situation. If a married woman is to use her gifts, abilities, and skills to benefit her own particular household, then it necessarily follows that every married woman is faced with a completely unique set of circumstances and must use creativity and innovation to "enflesh" the principles we have discussed: *subdue, fill, help,* and *glorify.* But each single woman is also faced with a completely unique set of circumstances, and just as much as the married woman, she too can think through the question of how she can best *subdue, fill, help,* and *glorify* in the place where she is standing.

Because every woman's situation is different, I hesitate to give examples lest it appear that I am prescribing some sort of universal to-do list when my whole point is that there *isn't* one overarching to-do list. On the other hand, without examples this could feel a bit abstract and hypothetical.

So let's imagine a woman who would love to be married, but in God's providence she just isn't. Some women in this situation simply hang around, hoping that someone will eventually show up. Others end up in the corporate world, more out of default than anything else. I would suggest that such a woman, although obviously in a challenging situation, can nonetheless be the kind of woman who creates in those around her a deep and fundamental loyalty to all the right things, who can use her gifts to show the *beauty* of holiness (Ps. 96:8) and to make truth *taste* (Ps. 34:8).

Maybe she starts a business, hires employees, and uses her talents as a way of blessing both them and her customers. Maybe she buys a house and throws herself into the role of homemaker and hostess, beautifying her surroundings and using her gifts to bless all who come through her door. A married woman with children has a built-in crowd that she needs to pour herself into—a single woman should look around her and figure out who the people are whom she can bless. No Christian should ever really be asking, "How can I fulfill myself?"—the question should always be pointed outward. *Who can I bless? How can I use my gifts to build up those around me? How can I embrace my femininity in such a way that I shine the light of the gospel into a lost and sinful world? How can*

I be truly excellent in the opportunities that God has placed in front of me? The answers will vary wildly, but the questions are always the same for every woman—married, single, old, young.

It's all good and well to claim those things, but how does it actually work out in the details? What are some of the ways this may actually look on the ground? Let's go back through the list of things we women were made to do, and try to put some flesh on it.

13.

SUBDUING MADE REAL

So we were made to work. To work hard. I think the first and easiest question to ask ourselves is whether we are actually doing that. Are our days challenging, difficult, tiring? They *ought* to be if we're living in obedience, but there are lots of ways to be busy and get tired without actually *working*. There are women whose days involve a whole lot of appointments and a lot of running back and forth, but when you look at the details of their busy schedule, they're actually running to the gym and then running out shopping and then running to the spa to get their nails done and then running out to coffee with girlfriends and then running out to dinner with a boyfriend and a lot of Instagramming in the off moments. A whole lot of busy and not a lot of work. This is the kind of woman whose highest aspiration is to be decorative and ornamental, a reheated twenty-first-century version of the

Victorian or 1950s ideal of a woman. A woman not capable of anything important or difficult, her main job is to keep herself looking good. Individual women can maintain that lifestyle, but as we've seen, women as a group can't handle it. Sooner or later the lid will blow off. As Christians, we should see that a woman who diligently devotes her days to nothing outside of the pursuit of her own beauty and enjoyment is a woman who is chasing the wind. There is no profit there, there is no fulfillment, there is no reward.

There are other women who technically get stuff done, but they aren't really working hard either. Maybe they're moms at home and their day is spent on Facebook in their sweats, putting some stuff in the dishwasher, dropping dinner in the crockpot, going to the park and chatting with friends for a couple hours, home for naps and more Facebook, fold some laundry, end of story. Stuff got done, yes. But not exactly challenging, difficult, fulfilling work. We live in an incredibly privileged time, and we don't have to kill ourselves just to survive. And this means that it becomes quite easy to decide to just float. If we don't have to run to survive, then why would we run? Why not take it easy and do the minimum? Why not live life exclusively in neutral or, at the very most, first gear?

But to whom much is given, much is required. Think again about Christ's parable of the talents. The master gave one servant five talents, another two talents, and the third servant received one talent. Then the master left, and the first two servants took the money and invested it. The one with five talents got a return of five talents, the one with two talents got a return of two, but the servant with only one talent buried his in the ground to save and give back to the master when he returned. When the master came back, the servants produced the money they had earned to return to him. The first two servants were rewarded with more, and the servant who had buried his talent was chastised and his one talent was taken away from him and given to one of the faithful servants. We twenty-first-century American women have been materially blessed far beyond the wildest dreams of most women throughout all of history. We are the ones who have been given the most talents, and God has given us the blessings in order that we may turn a profit on them. If we bury the talents and just float, we know what God says to us at the end of the day: "You wicked and slothful servant!" We need to look around at what God has given us and then figure out how to turn a profit on it. If we do that, we can look forward to a "Well done, good and faithful servant. You have been faithful over a little; I will set you over much. Enter into the joy of your master." So why should we run when we don't have to? Because that's what God made us to do. As Eric Liddell so eloquently says in *Chariots of Fire*, "God made me fast. And when I run I feel his pleasure."[1]

The next question to ask, beyond whether we're running at all, is what we're supposed to be pointed at. What you're

---

1. Well, technically the actor playing Eric Liddell said it. It's still a great line.

running *toward* is just as important a detail as the fact that you need to be running at all, and this is one of the places where feminism has led us astray. We have become accustomed to think that there's no room to run at home—if we want to throw ourselves at something meaningful, it needs to be "out there" in the world. Underachievers stay at home; women who want to do something with their lives go out into the workforce. But what does the Bible tell us that women should be aimed at? As we've seen, Titus 2 tells us that the older women should teach the younger to "love their husbands, to love their children, to be discreet, chaste, keepers at home, good, obedient to their own husbands, that the word of God be not blasphemed" (v. 5). The orientation, the direction the women should be pointed, is very clear. We should be pointed at our people—at our own husbands and children and homes. But our modern ears hear that and we instinctively feel a contradiction between the idea of "running" or "throwing ourselves" at something and the idea that we need to be pointed inward. "Doesn't focusing on our families mean that God has exiled us to a world with no scope? Where the most exciting thing we can look forward to is the trip to the grocery store?"

I would argue that this is a profound failure of imagination. When God says, "Here. I want you to work here," and hands us a house and a family, it's a shocking and embarrassing misunderstanding to think that He's just essentially tethered us with a very short leash to the brown microfiber sofa. When we conjure up the very uninspiring vision of beige, orange-peel-textured walls, Rubbermaid bins, Cheetos, and Crock-Pots, and think that's what we're doomed to, that's our own fault.

Have you ever noticed how terribly and hilariously overdramatized late-night infomercials can be? Perhaps they're advertising a plastic thingy for microwaving eggs. What they do is set up a little visual of what it *used* to be like, back before our lives were transformed by the plastic thingy. A woman comes into the kitchen and thinks about how she'd like to fix an egg. What must she do, then, but dig through a cabinet and unload the entirety of it as she looks for a pan. She staggers across the kitchen, carrying her armload of cookware, trips, staggers, drops the pans, breaks her toe, sweeps her arm across the counter as she falls, smashing all her best dishes, and ends up on crutches. And all because she didn't have the little handy plastic thingy! Oh, how our overall quality of life will improve if we will just purchase this egg-cooker! No more broken toes! Obviously the infomercial is not being overly concerned with accuracy in its portrayal of life without plastic egg cookers. The same is true when we conjure up a vision of life at home as gray and appallingly tedious. We're taking a caricature, absolutizing it, and then using that as a refutation of the whole idea. My husband has been a high school lacrosse coach for a number of years, and he has the same thing occur when he tries to teach a boy the right way to throw. Let's say a kid has bad throwing form that needs to be corrected. If he doesn't feel like correcting it, the usual technique is to hold the stick the way the coach told him to, do a dramatic stagger-throw demonstrating that when he does it the coach's way the ball goes straight into the ground and that's stupid. It's a big overdramatization of the situation to make the point that doing it the "right" way doesn't actually work. And that's what our culture has done with the stereotype of the wife and mother at home. Nothing interesting happens to a mom at home—unless you count her self-worth slowly dribbling away from her while she spends her days surrounded by ugliness and messes and boredom of the most excruciating kind.

But if we step out in faith, if we submit ourselves to God's commands and trust what we know of Him, we will actually find that the sky really is the limit when it comes to the kinds of things we can achieve. When we think of homemaking, we really need to think big. Think bigger than a vacuumed carpet. Think bigger than casseroles (Please!). Think bigger than a mid-century ideal where everything is superficially picture perfect and in its place. How can we take what God has given us and invest it, giving him a return on what's he's blessed us with?

The first thing we need to do is to stop trying to figure out how to make our jobs take less time so that we can have more time to lounge around. We should actually be asking how we can use all of that time we saved in order to *build* something. The technology we have access to makes it incredibly easy to spend very little time on the basics of living and then spend the rest of our days kicked back in neutral. But instead of being content with the bare minimum, what if we were to try to pursue excellence? What if, instead of looking for every possible way to cut corners, we were to look for every possible way to get better at our tasks?

Now, my thesis here is that there is truly unlimited scope for us to excel in the realm of homemaking, and again, I hesitate to give concrete examples lest it seem like I'm arguing there are only three ways to do this or something. I do sincerely believe that the field is wide, wide open before us, and if we women actually decided to apply our creativity and our imaginations to this question, we would see staggering results. But let me just throw a few things out there in the interest of trying to make this more practical.

What are the things that a woman at home spends time on? One obvious place is food. Everyone's hungry, and it's usually mom's job to make that problem go away. There are two ways of going about this.

The first is to feel bugged at everyone for being hungry again, darn it. So you feed them in a way that resolves the problem with the least amount of disruption to yourself. Maybe that means scouring the Internet for "impossibly easy recipes which require nothing more than a can opener" or buying prepackaged food that everyone can fix for themselves. Please note that I am not criticizing the food here, but the attitude. Prepackaged food can be used as a ridiculous blessing, and I am not trying to vilify either the food or everyone who makes use of it. But I am arguing that a sloppy, lazy, underachieving attitude is not glorifying to God and is not a joyful or fulfilling approach to life.

The second way to approach the problem of feeding everyone is to say to yourself, "This is a task that I have to do every single day—I had better figure out how to get good at it." So you start thinking through the significance of the task. You start asking questions like, "Why has God made us get hungry and have this need to eat every day? What does He want us to learn? How can I use this to teach my kids about God's goodness, His generosity, His grace, His overwhelming kindness, and use it to embody grace to my husband, my children, and my guests? How can I take this necessary task and use it to bless everyone in my house?" Maybe you grab some books by Father Capon and start thinking through the crazy beauty and significance of food and the task of feeding people. You decide to try and explore the absurd world of tastes and flavors that God has put all around us. You decide to learn about all the traditional cooking techniques that women have been using for centuries. You decide to make use of the ridiculous number of resources that surround us to actually attempt to *master* this job that you have to do every day anyway. You're curious. You want to never stop learning. You start trying to figure out the differences that different types of cookware make to the finished product and develop strong opinions about cast iron and copper. You decide to master the soufflé or the blintz. You decide to conquer the bread-making mountain. You go on a binge of braising meats to see what

your family likes best. You start reading up on weird vege-
tables that you can't buy at the grocery store and you decide
to grow them yourself and find out more about them.

Essentially you decide to use the task that's been put in
front of you as a way to learn more about God and the
breathtaking world He has put us in, a world with things
that come up out of the ground, for heaven's sake—things
with color and flavor and smell. Have you ever stopped
and thought about the sheer ridiculousness of the kind
of world we live in? I can step outside my door and put
two seeds in the dirt—the *dirt*—and one of them will
magically turn into a hot pepper plant which will produce bright red fruits to sear your tongue off—and the
other seed can magically give us a giant, bright orange
pumpkin. Where on earth did those seeds get that crazy color from anyway?! Where did it find that shocking
taste? How can a seed produce a giant purple onion out
of nothing but dirt and air and water? Why are basil and
tomatoes so stupidly good together? God could have put
us in a world where all food was brown and mushy, but
He didn't. He gave us textures and flavors and the insane
ability of heat to transform those flavors into something
different. Out of the hind ends of chickens He gives us
egg whites that fluff up into crazy meringue, which is
just downright silly. And out of cows He gives us milk
that can turn into butter or ice cream. And have you ever
thought about *that*? Before the sugar cane was noticed, ice
cream couldn't have been a thing, and chocolate wouldn't

have tasted good—both perfectly breathtaking pairings of flavors that no one had noticed yet (to say nothing of what happens when you combine the two). Or think about life before coffee! How sad would that have been? How many absolutely fabulous foods are out there still waiting to be invented, just waiting for the perfect magical combination of ingredients and techniques? God has made the world of food a world that is just *begging* to be explored, and He has actually made us with the need to eat food every single day if we want to survive. There's a wealth of possibilities there—and you could devote yourself to it for the rest of your life and not have even scratched the surface. So why not decide to approach your task with *that* attitude and see what difference it makes in your own heart and in your family?

What's another task that women at home are faced with? One obvious thing is clothing for everyone in the family. And again, there are always several ways to approach the question. One is to think of how we can do the least amount of work, and the other is to try and actually get good at our tasks. Clothing can sometimes seem like a trivial, or vain, or insignificant category . . . or on the other hand, it can seem like the only important subject in the world, depending on our personality type and general interests. So the big thing would be to turn to Scripture. What does God tell us about clothing, and what should our attitude be toward it? If this is something we have to do anyway, then it would be a good idea to figure out how God wants us to approach the subject. So we could turn to Proverbs 31 and see that the virtuous wife actually spends quite a bit of her time on clothing. She spins, she weaves, she clothes her household in scarlet, and she isn't afraid of the snow because she's spent time preparing for it. She makes herself clothing of silk and purple and tapestry, and not just for herself—she's actually so productive that she launches a business selling it (a successful one, apparently, because with her profits she buys real estate and plants a vineyard). What all this tells us is that clothing her family is a huge part of her effort and her time, and she takes care to get remarkably good at it. On the other hand, we're also told that she knows what's more important. She is clothed not just in scarlet and silk, but also in strength and honor. She knows the place that clothing is supposed to hold, and she knows how to not let it displace the more important things. But she also recognizes that this is not an either–or. She doesn't clothe herself in virtue and rags—she wears both virtue and *scarlet*. She puts focus and effort and time into the clothing, and the actual way that she does that is not at odds with her virtue but is rather the *evidence* of her virtue.

So how can we emulate that? How can we take that principle and bring it down to where we live? Do we shop exclusively at garage sales because we're scared of being worldly? Do we run up all the credit cards buying clothes we can't afford? Do we insist on wearing denim jumpers so as to not draw attention to ourselves? Do we think of nothing but Pinterest fashion boards from sunup to sundown? All of these would actually be ways of violating the scriptural principles of how a godly woman relates to the world of fashion. So maybe we could approach the question by asking ourselves what principles the Proverbs 31 woman embodies and then how we could translate that in our own situation and within our own budgets.

It's often surprising to me when I look at fashions from earlier generations—the amount of care and effort and skill that went into their everyday clothing is staggering compared to ours, and yet they did it with astonishingly fewer resources. Think of the craft that went into a woman's dress in the eighteenth century, back before there were sewing machines or factories or off-the-rack options, and before there were washing machines and dryers. If anyone ever had an excuse for living in yoga pants it was those women—and yet, somehow, they managed to completely outshine us in every possible way. Could Christian women actually pursue excellence in this field in a way that would change our cultural expectations? Not by awkwardly trying to copy women of the past (please no) but rather by trying to learn from them. By trying to take some of the effort and the craft and the appreciation of quality that went into fashion in earlier days and bring that across in a way that actually resonates now?

We could also ask questions about what clothing is for. Why do we assume that women with careers need to dress nicely but women at home don't? Where did that assumption come from? Is it correct or is it entirely wrong-headed? What should we do to change that? And why did God give us clothing in the first place? What problem is it solving and why? Is clothing meant to camouflage us or glorify us? What is immodesty, exactly, and why is it a problem? How can we avoid it without falling into the trap of thinking that our bodies are evil or embarrassing? How can we teach our girls to approach the whole subject of fashion? All of these are important, difficult, and profound questions that go far beyond the simple "oh that's so cute," which is where we can be tempted to stop.

Hopefully you can see that all those questions are actually fairly philosophical ones, questions that would take a lot of disciplined thinking to answer. Clothing your family could actually be a much bigger project than remembering to mark the Lands' End sale on your calendar. If Christian women seriously decided to approach this question at a fundamental level rather than a superficial and pragmatic one, we could expect to see some very interesting developments in the world of fashion.

The Proverbs 31 woman was not simply a consumer; she was a producer. She was a woman who was leaving her mark on her culture rather than simply letting the culture leave a mark on her. Let's be women who actually shape instead of always being the ones shaped, let's be the subjects and not always the direct objects, the movers rather than always the moved. To quote Henry V, "I cannot be confined within the weak list of a country's fashion. We are the makers of manners, Kate."[2] Why have we simply given up on the world of fashion and left that to the unbelievers as if this is something they should be in charge of? Could that ever be changed? If it's going to be, it would be the result of us Christian women making a conscious decision to be creators rather than mere consumers and throwing ourselves into the true pursuit of excellence in this field.

Another obvious area that homemakers are confronted with is the home itself. The house is an arena where we can feel the force of the parable of the talents very poignantly, because many of us are in homes that seem like a lost cause as far as beauty is concerned. Maybe you would love to have a beautiful, sprawling farmhouse, and all your Pinterest boards can attest to that fact—but you're actually in a stuffy little duplex, and it just feels like there's no point in even trying. Or maybe you have the big, beautiful, sprawling farmhouse, and there's nothing really that needs to be done to it, because it's already awesome. No matter what God has given us on this front, our job is to throw ourselves at it and turn a profit. To work, to run, to build, to glorify, and to transform. And if we actually did this we would discover that we will never really run out of scope. Let's say that you have the little duplex, so you give up and decide to wait for your ship to come in—you'll worry about making your home beautiful and inviting after you've won the lottery. That is nothing more than deciding

2. Shakespeare, *Henry V,* Act 5, Scene 2.

to bury your talent in the ground. What if you have no actual budget, so you decide to not try because you can't afford the furniture you'd like? Burying your talent. What if you have the house of your dreams, so you spend your days at the country club? Burying your talent. There are *always* ways for us to turn a profit on what God has put in front of us, and it really only requires creativity and an imagination that's ready to tackle the problem. Let's say that you're confronted with a house that's less than ideal in some way, or circumstances that make it difficult. It's tempting to give up and resent your lot in life, but actually, complication and difficulty are the soil in which true innovation and artistry grow. "Necessity is the mother of invention" is not just a truism, it's actually true. Michelangelo's David is sculpted from the hunk of marble that the other artists wouldn't touch because of the flaw that made it "impossible" to work with. If you have a situation that seems difficult, that means you'll have to attack it with real, true innovation and it will be a real, true challenge. But remember that "the essence of every picture is the frame," and that a real challenge is also a real opportunity for satisfaction in your work. If it were simple and easy, it would just be boring.

But why should we care about our homes? Why should they be beautiful? What does that matter anyway? To answer those questions we should once again go back to Scripture. As we've already discussed, we like to think, "Tending the home is petty and demeaning work—why is God asking women to do it? He must hate us and Paul is obviously a misogynist." But the more faithful approach is to look at the command and say, "God wants women to tend the home—tending the home must therefore be a hugely meaningful task." The way we respond to the command shows whether we trust God or whether we doubt Him. Whether we assume He has great things in store for us or whether we assume that He prefers to hoard up nasty surprises to slap us with. It's good for us to go through this again: If God is good, and if He wants us to subdue this planet, and if He wants us to obey the Great Commission and conquer this world for Christ, and if He tells half the human race that they're in charge of tending the home, it follows from this that the home is actually one of the most strategic and important tools by which the world will be won. We should not read that command as God telling the women to get out of the way and make room for the important stuff—He's telling them to get out there on the front lines. If a soldier is told to go to his place in the battle and he instead shuffles off somewhere else, muttering about his self-worth, the one thing we can't accuse him of is being excessively courageous. When women, as a group, left their battle stations and wandered away, the one thing we can't say about them is that they were being bold and fearless.

The home clearly matters, and matters a lot. And why is that? The home is the beating heart that powers everything else. The home nurtures, feeds, provides rest, gives shelter, and creates a loyalty to itself that is one of the strongest and most compelling of all human emotions. Home is where your people are, and all of your deepest loves and allegiances are wrapped up in it. Or at least they can be. Home can also be a place of bitterness, heartache, betrayal, and hatred, a place of emptiness and loneliness, a place where things are taken, not given, a place that creates a gaping wound in the souls of those who belong to it. It can weave together or it can shatter, and the person at the helm is the woman. Whatever else you may say about it, it's not an irrelevant position to hold.

So how can we use the home to create deep loyalty in our people? I can think of lots of ways to *not* do it: by spending our days complaining about how awful it all is, by acting like it's not worth bothering about, by taking no time and putting in no effort, by doing the bare minimum, by actively despising our own roles, by acting like working on the home is the worst punishment that could be inflicted on anybody, by living life in a frumpy house with a frumpy attitude. We could also make home a living hell for everyone by getting caught up in the home for its own sake and forgetting what it's there for: by creating a beautiful home full of things no one can touch—furniture you can't sit on, toys kept on the highest shelves where they won't make a mess—a house that looks picture perfect but where nobody wants to be. You can use beauty to drive people away as well as to draw people in, and it all depends on what it's aimed at. Does the beauty exist for its own sake and the people just get in the way? Or does the beauty exist for the sake of the people who are meant to enjoy it? C.S. Lewis says, "To desire the *desiring* of her own beauty is the vanity of Lilith, but to desire the *enjoying* of her own beauty is the obedience of Eve."[3] What is the beauty there for? For itself or for another? A frumpy and unhappy home will drive people away, but so will a beautiful and unhappy home.

On the other hand, we women could instead use our position as homemakers to create homes that are utterly compelling. Where the love and the delight and the joy and the gratitude for all of God's blessings are translated into how a table is set, how the walls are painted, how the rooms invite you to come in and enjoy them. Where everything about it preaches a sermon on the *goodness* of God and the joy He takes in the smallest details. There's not one square inch of God's creation that doesn't reflect His artistry and His delight in beauty. We can either copy Him in that, and attempt to use our homes to testify to God's abundant and overwhelming delight in beauty, or we can use our homes to say the opposite—that nothing matters and it's all stupid and nobody cares anyway.

Maybe the thought of trying to create a home like that is daunting—maybe decorating isn't your forte. Well, we actually live in the midst of an embarrassment of riches when it comes to resources and opportunities to learn and get better at virtually any subject we want to tackle. No one can ever say that they've figured it all out, they've learned

---

3. C.S. Lewis, *That Hideous Strength* (New York: Scribner, 1996), 63.

it all, there's nothing left to do. There's always more interest that we can earn on our talents—it just takes a bit of initiative and a willingness to learn.

This is seriously just scratching the surface of three areas—out of a host of possibilities. I don't have time to list the myriad other categories that give women scope to excel—gardening, poetry, music, hospitality, lovemaking, educating, art, design, and so, so many more. There are so many ways that women could go if they decided to truly pursue the domestic arts—and decided to actually treat them as if they were *arts* and not embarrassing, demeaning, menial tasks or trite little crafts and hobbies.

One other thing already mentioned but worth remembering is that just because a woman is oriented *toward* the home does not mean that she may never venture *out* of the home. When Titus says that women should be keepers of the home, it's important to realize that a home is bigger than the walls of the house. The home is made up of the *people* that house shelters, and that is where the true focus needs to be. Because of that, there are many ways in which a woman could work *outside* the home in a way that makes the home itself more potent, more glorious, more compelling. The Proverbs 31 woman was oriented toward the home—so much so that it spilled out into successful business ventures outside. But in that case her business was an overflow from her home, not something which sucked the home dry. It was a way of giving to her family, not a way of taking away from them. The question is not where a woman is standing but which direction she is pointed.

Friedan's thesis was that in order for a woman to achieve true fulfillment in her calling she needed to turn her back on the home and on children. But I would submit that if we women decided to take our motivation, our drive, our inspiration, our imagination, and our creativity, and aim it *toward* our homes, our husbands, and our children, we would find a vast and glorious and transformative world of possibilities open up before us.

14.

FILLING MADE REAL

Alongside the command to subdue the earth is the command to fill it. Fruitfulness and fertility are what Eve was created for. This obviously applies directly to children, and I believe that there are a whole lot of Christian women out there who need to rethink their opinions on this subject. Many are frightened by the whole project because having children is a huge invasion of yourself at the most fundamental level, and that's just plain scary. Having a baby messes up your figure, gives you stretch marks, is undoubtedly painful, and your body, without your consent, begins to prioritize the needs of another human over your own. Another person moves in and takes over your body, and then they come out, but they don't leave. They are now a part of you forever. You don't just get pregnant and then nine months later you're done. That child is an eternal soul, and will forever be a part of your story, even if you lose the baby or give it up for adoption and never see it again. Another person has imprinted on your soul and you'll never be the same. This is a huge deal. And it's scary. And *painful*. And all that. Yes, you will lose yourself. But nonetheless, that's what God created us to do, and if we refuse to put the seed in the ground we'll never see the flower. If we won't accept the death, we'll never see the glory. But if you lay yourself down in the fertile soil of obedience and faith, God will use that to bring forth fruit, thirty, sixty, and a hundredfold.

Of course fruitfulness is not limited to the simple act of childbearing. There's so much more to it than that—and women who are never able to have children can yet be staggeringly fruitful in many other areas. And even in the realm of physical childbearing, pure quantity has never been the point. We are told in Malachi, "And did not he make them one? Yet had he the remnant of the spirit. And why one? That he might seek a godly offspring" (Mal. 2:15). God doesn't just need women cranking out babies. He desires *godly* offspring, and that requires an awful lot more than just nine months of pregnancy and a successful delivery. Populating the earth with a lot of little heathens is not the picture of obedient fruitfulness, and it would be a mistake to think that women were brought into the picture with the goal of simply producing a lot of generic humans. Having fifteen rebellious children is not a spiritual win. God desires a godly offspring, and that doesn't happen by accident, and it doesn't happen automatically. Part of our calling to fruitfulness involves bringing up our children "in the nurture and admonition of the Lord" (Eph. 6:4), and that is a full-contact undertaking, not something you can do if you only bump into your children occasionally between business trips.

But you also cannot do it if you refuse to have any children at all. Now, it goes without saying that if God has not given you children, whether because you are single or because you've never been able to conceive, *of course* you can still be fruitful, glorious, productive, and blessed by God in your femininity and in your calling. There's nothing inherently blessed about the physical act of childbearing. A woman can have children to the glory of God or in defiance of God, and a woman can be childless to the glory of God or in defiance of God.

I am concerned right now with the women in that last group—women who despise the fruitfulness which God has blessed them with, women who call that blessing a curse and who refuse to die to themselves in order that someone else might live. That attitude is found at its most potent form in the radical feminist movement in America where it has been embedded for over a century, but the aroma of it has wafted into many Christian marriages. Many Christian women don't want to have children until they've "had a life" first, but all the underlying assumptions in that decision are shaped by a radical feminism which, to their credit, they would probably reject if they saw it in its pure form. For instance, as one lesbian blogger put it, "We are not here to 'breed' for 'breeding' does little more than reinforce women's role as the caregiver, nurturer. By having children we harm our careers, make ourselves vulnerable to attack and abuse, and become reduced to unpaid labour."[1] Or, in an editorial piece on why choosing childlessness is admirable, not selfish, a feminist author says, "A society that prioritizes pleasure and self-worth sounds a whole lot better than one that valorizes denial, unnecessary sacrifice and general resignation at the way things are (at least for women)."[2] Many Christians would raise their eyebrows a little at saying those things quite that bluntly, but they would still base all their personal decisions on a notion that once a woman has gotten pregnant, she has just become irrelevant, marginalized, and taken out of the game. They don't see motherhood as a world of opportunities opening up, but rather as a world of opportunities closing in their faces. Our culture has come to despise fruitfulness so much that we Christians sometimes don't see how far it has crept into our own thinking as well. But if God says the opposite (and He does) then our duty is to trust Him and to step out in faith and obedience to a command that, yes, can look daunting and scary. But the good news is that when we trust God, He's never waiting at the other end to say,

---

1. @planetcath, "The Breeders," Motherhood Is a Feminist Issue, https://miafi .wordpress.com/2014/09/27/the-breeders (accessed Feb. 24, 2016). This was actually written by a lesbian mother defending the fact that she had had a child at one point.

2. Jill Filipovic, "The choice to be child-free is admirable, not selfish," *The Guardian*, http://www.theguardian.com/commentisfree/2013/aug/16/choice-child-free -admirable-not-selfish (accessed Feb. 24, 2016).

"Haha, tricked you!" God is faithful, and He gives what He promises. Obedience and faith never turn out to have been a trap.

But women are called to be fruitful in many ways, not just in the physical act of childbearing. We aren't just meant to fill the world with humans; we are commanded to fill the earth with the knowledge of the Lord as the waters cover the sea (Matt. 28:18–20; Hab. 2:14; Isa. 11:9). And since the Great Commission was given to the church, not just to the men, the women obviously have a huge role to play here. But what is it? How can we be fruitful in this area?

The Bible is pretty clear that one role women are *not* to fill is that of preacher or elder in the church, and this has caused a great deal of angst amongst women who would like to be both Christians and feminists. Paul really could not be clearer on the subject: "I do not permit a woman to teach or have authority over a man" (1 Tim. 2:12). This unfortunate bluntness of his has kicked up a huge amount of dust. It has also treated us to a vast array of complicated and gymnastical studies of the Greek and Ancient Near Eastern context, by which feminist biblical "scholars" have managed to prove that when Paul says he does not permit a woman to teach or have authority, what he *actually* means is that women are most definitely supposed to teach and have authority. "If you don't understand the argument then you obviously have not read my thesis on the subject, which is very, very scholarly and also scholarly." But if we are women who care even a little bit about being intellectually honest, we have to square up to the fact that we're not allowed to be pastors. So there's that. Pastoral teaching positions are out. And in the grand scheme of things, that's not exactly high-handed tyranny and oppression. Women who have their feelings hurt by this really need to get out more and see that there are, as a matter of fact, people in the world with actual problems.[3]

But if we're not to be church leaders, then what meaningful contribution could we make to the mission of the church? There are the obvious answers to this, answers that everyone knows, but I actually want to go a bit beyond that. The self-evident things that we've all thought of already are things like women taking care of the poor, showing hospitality, and being evangelistic. But I want to push it out a bit further than that and say that it's not just in those moments that we help the cause, but also that our role in the day-to-day life in the home is absolutely vital to the spread of the gospel. And this is why.

When men bring about change, they usually do it by fiat. They decide how something is going to be, they lay it out clearly, and then they expect people to conform to it. It's very linear and direct, and it's a vital and necessary role. But women have another way of effecting change, and that is by making something attractive. Making it lovely. This is what we're geared for, what we were created

---

3. If this is the first time you're hearing all this, you can find a more complete treatment of the question in Douglas Wilson, *Why Ministers Must Be Men* (Monroe, LA: Athanasius Press, 2010).

for, what we're good at, and what we love. And it's incredibly powerful, either for good or for evil. How many men have been led astray from everything they say they believe by the wrong beautiful woman? How many men have had their loyalties and their virtues cemented and anchored and made firm by the right beautiful woman? Beauty is a powerful and compelling force that draws people, and I don't just mean personal beauty or sexual attraction, but beauty in every part of life. Art, music, food, poetry, nature—beauty tugs at a deeper part of ourselves than our intellect. And our job as women is to take the abstract, the cerebral, the intellectual, and make it lovely, make it beautiful, make it attractive.

Being a woman is in many ways like being in the field of applied mathematics—except that it's applied theology, applied philosophy. We are the ones who take the metaphysical principles, the heady and complicated truths of our faith, and instead of *saying* it to the men in a sermon we *show* it to them. Our job is to make holiness beautiful, to make it *taste*. We draw people to the truth by showing them the beauty of life in Christ, and in real, actual, tangible ways. If theology is a river, women dig the canals that bring the water into every part of the garden. Righteous women preach the truth, but in parable, metaphor, incarnate poetry. What the pastors explain with words, women sing with hot food, with wine, with welcoming homes, with love and joy that spills out into everything they touch and that draws people irresistibly to the truth that is being embodied.

It's not that men are supposed to be involved in teaching theology and women aren't—it's that men are to teach it one way and women are to teach it another. If men are the words, women are the music. If men are the skeleton, women are the flesh. If men are the radio waves, women are the amplifiers. It has nothing to do with saying that women aren't smart enough, or tough enough, or gifted enough, or anything of the kind. But God loves harmony. He loves the same tune playing out in different strains of the music, intertwining, harmonizing, and each making the other more powerful by virtue of the fact that each is doing something different than the other. God is writing a song with harmony, and the feminists want to insist that everyone stay on the same note all the time. If truth were a salted caramel, the feminists would like to take away the caramel and just serve the salt.

In the notorious passage in 1 Timothy 2 where Paul prohibits women from teaching, I think it's quite striking that he also discusses how she should learn. Everyone gets wound up in a snarl about the fact that she should learn "in silence," but what they fail to notice is that she's *learning*. Paul is assuming that women are to be students of the Word, and there's never a hint that it's more important for the men to be educated in the faith than the women. Women are prohibited from *preaching* theology, but it's never assumed that they shouldn't *know* theology. And we don't learn important truths so that we can keep the knowledge to ourselves, locked away in our brains for our own personal edification, but rather so that we can take that truth and then translate it into everything we do. If our job is to take the complicated truths of orthodoxy and preach them by means of food and upholstery and clothes and sex and bedtime stories and childbirth and flower arrangements, then I would submit that having a good handle on our theology is a *must*.

Our job as women—and it's a phenomenal responsibility—is to enflesh the weighty truths of our faith. If our role is to make truth *taste*, to make holiness *beautiful*, then what does that look like in the details? As a random example of this, take Christmas. Christmas is, of course, when God did ultimately what we women can only shadow. The ultimate enfleshing. At Bethlehem, God's Word became flesh and dwelt among us, the Consolation of Israel was born of a woman—and that moment was so staggering that even the stars had to come down and see it. And then, every year, we celebrate that moment. We take one of the most difficult theological truths—the Incarnation—and attempt to show that truth through our celebrations. The men can talk about the Incarnation, church fathers can write important treatises about it, pastors can preach about it, theologians can parse and define it . . . but we women are the ones who make it taste like something. We make it smell good. How crazy is that? "And for my next trick, I will take Athanasius' *De Incarnatione* and I will say it with cookies and wrapping paper and cinnamon and marshmallows and colored lights and tablecloths and shopping trips and frantically-last-minute-late-night-Amazon-orders and ham—and I will do it in such a way that my four-year-old will really *get* it, and it will send roots deep down into his soul where it will anchor his loves and his loyalties and shape his allegiances well into his nineties."

Femininity is powerful and it is persuasive and it is compelling. The premier example of this is actually given to us in the very next couple of verses of 1 Timothy 2. We are told several things: that women are to learn in silence, that they may not teach or have authority over a man, that Adam was formed first and then Eve, and that "Adam was not deceived, but the woman being deceived was in the transgression" (v. 14). I'm not sure the main point here is that women are less good at critical thinking or too gullible to be allowed to teach (although that interpretation is certainly hard to deny when we glance at the ranks of women who are trying to argue they should be pastors—"Gullible" and "Incapable of Critical Thinking" appear to be the two main planks of their party platform). But to return to the point I find incredibly interesting—this verse comes right on the heels of telling us that the woman needs to *learn*. Why should she learn? Why does it matter that she be educated in the faith? If we can just get past our indignation about *how* she should learn, it might behoove us to ask why Paul thinks it's important that she learn at all… And I do think he answers that question: It's because when Eve was deceived and believed the wrong thing, look at the incredible destruction it caused. Eve was deceived—her intellect fell into error—but that wasn't Adam's problem in that moment. He wasn't deceived at all—but he went with Eve anyway. His brain wasn't confused, but Eve— even in error—is powerful and compelling. A woman who has gotten ahold of an incorrect belief is still dangerously persuasive; she still wields enormous influence, even if the man knows perfectly well better. It is absolutely vital that women be well versed in the faith, because if the women are not, I'm afraid the men are in trouble as well—even if all their theological ducks are, for the moment, in a row. So it is utterly vital that women be superbly educated—an ignorant woman may just be one of the most lethal dangers on the planet.

Too often conservative housewives actually agree with the feminists. The feminists have argued that homemaking is a brainless job, requiring no actual education or skill and making no significant impact on the world—and they have run away from it. But many actual homemakers, those who have embraced that life for whatever reason, also treat it like a brainless job, requiring no actual education or skill and making no significant impact on the world. I have heard extremely conservative people actually suggest that their daughters didn't need as much education as their sons because they were just going to get married and have babies—they didn't need a job, so obviously school wasn't really important. Or a more mainstream version of that is to suggest that a daughter needs to be given an education *in case* she never gets married or she loses her husband or something—"She needs to have something to fall back on if she needs to support herself." I truly don't think that even the most ardent feminist could be more insulting to homemaking than that.

My brother is a fellow at a small, extremely rigorous, Christian liberal arts college called New Saint Andrews that also happens to be my alma mater. Students study, among other things, theology, philosophy, rhetoric, history, literature, Latin, Greek, art, natural philosophy, and music. The workload is stiff, the expectations are high, and the one-on-one oral finals with professors are intimidating. It's definitely not the place to come if you're looking for a nice, soft four years of hanging out and playing Frisbee. Because of the demanding nature of the education, it can sometimes be easy for the girls to get tired and start wondering why, again, they thought this was a good idea (well, and the guys too, if it comes to that). But especially if all the girl really wants to do is get married and have a family, it can be easy to start fussing about the workload, feeling like all these fat books and difficult concepts are making her head hurt for no good reason, and wishing she could chuck it all and depart for the blissful world of homemaking where, apparently, she will never have to think again. Whenever my brother's students would begin to exhibit signs of this attitude, he would listen to their outpouring of woe, tell them he really sympathized, and offer to help them out. He said he would make them t-shirts that they could wear around to their classes—t-shirts that would say in large letters across the back, "For Breeding Purposes Only." Now—in the above scenario, who is being insulting to homemaking? I'll give you a hint—it isn't my brother. Fundamentally, girls who can't see how education will benefit them as homemakers are actually on the same page as the most hard-core of feminists, believing that a brain is a waste if you're "only" going to be a wife and mother.

Other conservatives react against that kind of thing and they try to make homemaking seem like really important work. And while I applaud the sentiment in the abstract, the ways in which they attempt to do it are frequently excruciatingly patronizing and not at all helpful. When a woman starts seriously describing her daily duties in the vocabulary of the corporate world, it just comes off as if she's a sad wannabe career woman who had something go wrong somewhere, so she's had to resort to playing dress-up and pretending to be important. I'm talking about describing yourself as, "Chief Sanitation Expert, Regional Transportation Coordinator, Culinary Director, and Chief Executive of the Home." That actually is not helping anything when it comes to the perception that homemakers have sad little lives. Our jobs are *not* important because they keep us just as busy as if we had "real" careers. They're not important because we can come up with important sounding words to describe them. Our jobs are important because they are *poetry*. Because they shape loves and they shape loyalties, they teach and they convict. They're important because they take glorious truths and make them incarnate, make them visible, and weave them into the souls of the people around us.

What do I mean exactly when I say that our jobs are poetry? Think for a moment about the power of a well-crafted poetic line. The potency of poetry lies in its ability to take a large, complicated, wordy concept, and then cram it into a few, well-chosen lines which communicate the same thing, only better. Look at these lines from Alexander Pope.

> A little learning is a dang'rous thing;
> Drink deep, or taste not the Pierian spring:
> There shallow draughts intoxicate the brain,
> And drinking largely sobers us again.[4]

Now let me try to say the same thing, capturing all the same concepts, only this time in prose. How's this:

> It's dangerous to be only a little bit educated, because when you're only a little bit educated you don't realize how little your education actually is, and you can get carried away with your own wisdom in much the same way that you can get drunk—except the odd part is that when you get drunk, it's because you have partaken too much, and in the case of education, the drunkenness comes because you haven't partaken enough. And what you're partaking of is the fount of wisdom, which I could describe as the fount of the Muses, since they are the source of

---

4. Alexander Pope, "An Essay on Criticism" (1711), Part 2, lines 15–18.

knowledge in Greek mythology. That's the fountain from which it's important to drink deeply in order to be sober, because if you drink from it just barely you will be drunk—not on wisdom but on your own ignorance. So the fountain of knowledge is like alcohol except in reverse.

Whew. Wordy and tedious. But now go back and read Alexander Pope's version again. It says all that—but it says it beautifully. It says it in a way which makes you think about it, wonder about it, chew on it, and unpack it. And when we're done, we can go back and read it again and still enjoy it, because the poetry is lovely. In fact, the beauty of the poetry is what makes us feel like attempting to unpack it in the first place—and no one would ever feel like reading my prose version again, even if they could make themselves concentrate through it the first time.

In a similar way, women are uniquely gifted at being able to take a wordy, dry, abstract concept—and then weave it into incarnate poetry, making it something that people want to come back to again. I love how the queens are portrayed in Anglo-Saxon literature, and it illustrates this concept well. For the warrior culture of the Saxons, the mead hall was the center of their universe. It was where all the men came together to drink mead, to feast, to listen to the songs of the bard, and to receive their rewards from the king. They sat on benches in the great hall, and it was the queen who brought the mead to the warriors, serving them from a giant horn. As she made her way through the hall, serving the men, she gave them gifts, rewards from the king for their valor in battle. She distributed the gold, and reminded them of their duties and their vows of allegiance. As she wove her way through the hall, she was weaving the men together around the tables, cementing their loyalties to one another and to the common cause. Think how much more effective that is than sending them a form in the mail, reminding them of the clauses in their contracts or making everyone attend a seminar with a Power Point presentation. Food, fellowship, laughter, beauty—these form loyalties that run deep.

My mother has set an incredibly powerful example in this regard. I have one brother and one sister, and as we were growing up and moving out, my parents invited us to come to their house every Saturday night for a Sabbath dinner. There was no pressure—no hint of "you have to come or we'll be offended"—simply an invitation to a big, lovely meal of food and wine and fellowship every Saturday. It quickly became a part of the week that was nonnegotiable for us kids. It's gotten to the point that we'll plan our trips as much as possible to make sure we don't miss Sabbath dinner. There were six of us around the table when we started, and now my mother cooks dinner every Saturday for the eight adults and seventeen grandchildren of our immediate family, plus a load of welcome extras. Without any extra guests, our base number every week is thirty-five. My children have grown up sitting around a table every week with seventeen cousins plus aunts and uncles and grandparents and their great-grandfather. The kids have wine in their glasses to toast the coming Lord's Day, and the evening is full of amazing food and laughter and chaos and messes and stories and political discussions and cousins-versus-uncles dodgeball (dubbed "Uncleball") in the summer evenings. As I look around every Saturday night at the sea of laughing cousin faces, I see deep allegiances forming and loyalties cementing in my mother's mead hall. These are bonds which will run very, very deep, and they are formed through the sacrificial love of my mother, love that you can smell as soon as you open the door of your car in the driveway, love that looks like a beautiful table, love that tastes like meat and potatoes and gravy, love that you can hear in the chatter of happy voices, laughing over the food and the wine, love you can feel in the warmth of the crackling fire and the welcoming hugs.

When the Word became flesh and dwelt among us, that Incarnation was the salvation of the world. In a much smaller way, on a smaller scale, women are called to take the Word and then make it flesh—how could that not be incredibly powerful and transformative? How could we look at our task and think it's demeaning, or brainless, or small, or a distant second fiddle to the men's assignment? How could we see that opportunity and then fuss because we wanted to stand in the pulpit or sit in a cubicle instead?

15.

HELPING MADE REAL

Eve was created as a helper for Adam, and we've already seen how that should be read not as an inferior role but rather as a hugely significant and powerful one. But it's also a bit relative. "Women" are not called to help "men," but rather each woman is meant to help her own husband. And since each man is different and has a different vocational calling, that means that each woman's job will be completely unique. There is no checklist or Pinterest printable that captures the daily duties of every godly wife. This is not simplistic, and it requires a good bit of wisdom and creativity and ability to translate and apply the principles to our own situations. Luckily, however, that very much plays to our feminine strengths.

Years ago, my husband and I bought a terrible old beater of a farmhouse and began remodeling it. We gutted the kitchen completely and were starting from scratch on it. As we were figuring out what we wanted the new kitchen to look like, I began showing Ben pictures to see if I could get a feel for his tastes, since up to that point we had been in rental homes and had not had the option of creating something that really reflected *us*. I kept gravitating toward all-white kitchens, but Ben didn't seem to like any of them. He's a guy who knows what he likes but doesn't have a single interior decorator bone in his body, so he never really explained why he didn't like them or what it was about them that bothered him. Obviously I wanted to create a kitchen that we both loved, but I was having a hard time figuring out what exactly it was that made him react the way he did. And then one day he said it. I showed him a beautiful white kitchen, all gloss and marble and sunlight and general fabulousness . . . and he said, "I don't like kitchens that look like they would smell like cleaner. I think the kitchen should look like it smells like hot food in the oven." That was it. The key. Something with handles that I could run with. Yeah, it was vague. Making something *look* like it would *smell* like something hot and delicious . . . not exactly a concrete description. But it was all I needed. I just needed to be pointed in the right direction and then I could take that and translate. I could turn that into paint choices and wood finishes, and we were able to create a kitchen that both of us completely loved.

And that's what each of us women needs to do when figuring out how to be a helper to her own particular man.

We need to take something a bit abstract and then translate it. Each of us has a completely different project on our hands, and we need to figure out how to be obedient in our own unique circumstances. What does it look like to help, to sacrifice, to glorify, and to be fruitful if your husband is a plumber who likes to hunt and hates parties? It looks completely different than if he were a beekeeper who likes crossword puzzles and gardening, or an academic who enjoys opera and dinner parties. Every man is unique, and being a helper to him means that you have to translate—to take an abstract principle and translate it into something tangible. Just because one woman shows her love for her husband by giving him exotic food does not automatically mean that it would be a blessing to your husband if he really would just prefer tuna melts.

The principle in each case is the same, but we will each translate it in our own way. Have you ever seen a woman who dresses for the body she wishes she had and not the body she in fact has? It's always painful to witness. And in the same way, we need to be helpers to the man we actually have and not the man we think he ought to be. We need to translate. Make the principles real in our own situations. Look at your husband, look at his calling, look at his loves, and then glorify it. Throw yourself into the project. If he is an electrician, make that glorious—and I guarantee that you can do it. Make your children see that their dad is amazing, that his work is significant, and that they are incredibly privileged to be a part of it. A random, well-known example of someone doing this is the Pioneer Woman. She's taken her role as the wife of a cattle rancher and she has glorified it. She revels in the fact that her husband is out there in the mud with the cows, but it would have been just as easy for her to get all embarrassed of what he does and wish he had a job in the city with health benefits. She has thrown herself into her part in a way that's absolutely admirable. On the other hand, just because she blogs about her husband's work does not mean that your own husband would appreciate you doing that about his. He may not be thrilled with you taking pictures of him in his cubicle and blogging about how hot you think he is in that new sweater vest. You have to translate, not copy. You have to look at your own situation and use wisdom, creativity, discernment. Take the abstraction and then make it real, make it glorious. Put flesh on it.

What does your husband love? How does he like to spend his time? How does he want his children raised? Figure it out, and then run with that. Make it happen, and make it happen in a way that takes his breath away—a way that he could never have achieved alone. And don't look at what the other women are doing unless you're going to translate it before incorporating the idea—don't try to be the helper to a husband you don't have. That would just be trying to be the knife when what's required is a can opener.

This may seem a bit undignified. The idea of trying to help a man instead of pursuing your own dreams feels a bit embarrassing, particularly if the husband you're confronted with doesn't seem like an especially rewarding project. But remember that this is transformative. Women change the world this way. Wives are told in 1 Peter that they are capable of winning their husbands without a word—and that's because we can be compelling, powerful, and persuasive without it (1 Pet. 3:1). If wives returned to their battle stations in this way, I think they would find that their husbands would suddenly start performing a whole lot better themselves.

But what if you have no husband? What if there's no specific personality who sets the brackets around your calling? Does that mean that there's no place for you, no meaningful work available to you? Of course not! Think for a second about the significance of the land of Israel in the Old Testament. The incredible gift that God gave to His people was that land, and think how much of the law is taken up with how that land is to be allotted, inherited, and handed down. An inheritance in the land was hugely meaningful and very much at the core of what it meant to be an Israelite. But then God set aside a special people for himself, the Levites, and said, "Thou shalt have no inheritance in their land, neither shalt thou have any part among them: *I am thy part and thine inheritance* among the children of Israel" (Num. 18:20). The Levites had no inheritance in the land because their inheritance was God himself, and this was not a situation where the Levites were being given a lousy deal. Being called to be a wife is a huge privilege and a huge undertaking with a huge significance, but if God has not given you an inheritance in the land it is because He Himself is your inheritance. You have a different set of challenges in front of you and a different set of blessings, but your job is the same. You take the truth of the gospel and you translate it into beautiful and compelling and incarnate life which preaches the goodness of God to everyone surrounding you. Every Christian woman is called to this, regardless of her particular station in life.

16.

GLORIFYING MADE REAL

Have you ever noticed how invitations to formal events specify the dress code in terms of what the men will wear? You may be invited to a black tie event, but no one expects the women to be in a black tie—it is simply assumed that they will know how to translate. When we lived in Oxford we were invited frequently to events with strict dress codes—and I had to understand that if my husband was instructed on the invitation to wear a suit, that translated to a nice dress for me but definitely not a gown. On the other hand, if he was told to be in a white tie, a gown was nonnegotiable. "Smart casual" had very distinct expectations for the men—and then the women translated into something comparable but feminine. In each of these cases the men wear what is literally spelled out with very little flexibility—and the women embody the principle, but they each do it in their own way. At a black tie event, all the men look the same, but the women are all proclaiming "black-tie-ness" in completely unique ways, none of which actually involves a black tie. And what is striking to me about this is that when everyone looks at pictures later, it's the women's outfits they want to see. No one cares about what the men had on—the red carpet photos are all about the women. So the invitation gives the rule to the men—but what everyone actually wants to know is what the women are going to do with that. How will the women take the "rule" and then glorify it?

Now imagine if women started getting offended that they weren't mentioned on the invitations. What if they started insisting that they be given equal airtime in dress code specifications? What if they complained that they should be allowed to wear black ties like the men and be treated completely equally? We would immediately lose interest in what the women were wearing, because it would immediately be boring. If they all started showing up to parties wearing strict tuxedos just like the men, it would be just about the most dismal scene I can imagine. As soon as women start demanding "equality" at the top of their lungs they kill the glory, because the essence of glory is dependent on *difference*. Imagine a poignant, bone-chilling vocal harmony—and then imagine what would happen to it if the equality police came in to insist that everyone sing on the same note instead. We have to be willing to embrace the fact that women are different from men. We are called to different things than the men, we've been created to do different tasks than the men, we've been gifted differently than the men—and if we embrace that truth we will find ourselves able to sing in harmony, able to glorify.

And that's what we do, after all. We glorify. We are made both to *be* glory and to *multiply* that glory in the small things and in the great things. Fundamentally, we show and become that glory when we submit freely to one who is our equal, when we give ourselves, sacrifice ourselves for others, and that glory is a flame which grows and spreads. It is a city on a hill that cannot be hidden. It is a light which shines before men who see our good works and then glorify our Father who is in heaven (Matt. 5:16). It is a glory which points to the greater glory, a candle next to the sun.

But this is a glory which will only grow if we are pointed at something outside of ourselves, if our loves and our desires are focused on something else, if we are able to lay ourselves down for another. The glory dies when we begin looking at ourselves, at our needs, at our rights, at our self-esteem, at our fulfillment. If we grasp for those things, if we grab and clutch at our own dignity, we will surely lose it. Whoever tries to save his life will lose it. But whoever is willing to lose his life, for Christ's sake, will find it.

When we lay on the altar that which is dearest to us, when we bury it in the ground, God gives it back it to us, glorified. If we lay our pride down, He gives us incredible dignity. If we lay our dreams down, He gives us unspeakable fulfillment. When we bury our own ambitions, He returns them back to us with interest. That which we put in the ground is a shriveled little seed, and what God hands back to us is a gorgeous handful of flowers—not a bad trade. So we need to stop feeling self-conscious that we've lost our seed. When we look at our plant that is covered in blooms, we need to not feel sheepish if the well-dressed and successful career woman holds out her hand and shows us that she still has her little seed. (And, again, is "well-dressed and successful career woman" even an accurate picture of the average woman's job outside of the land of TV make-believe? That glamorous dream is often very far from most working women's reality.) When the culture sneers at us for having so foolishly laid our seed in the dirt, when they pity us for having dropped that precious, withered, brown pellet instead of clutching it in our sweaty little palms, we need to turn and look at the blooms and thank God for His mercy that allowed us to let go.

Feminine glory is fruitful. It produces. It builds. It creates. And it does so in ways that are profound and staggering and surprising and beautiful and frequently messy and hilarious and ridiculous. Fruit is never, ever tidy, and building things always makes a mess—so keep your eye on the harvest and realize that in this world God made, the mud is an essential ingredient. Think about the finished house and realize that the sawdust is a given. Remember that the stall is clean where there is no ox, but much increase comes by the strength of an ox (Prov. 14:4). As we build, as we glorify, as we try to imitate God in our fruitfulness, we should make sure that our vision for what that will look like is shaped by what God Himself has shown us, and not what minimalist lifestyle magazines claim the beautiful life is. On the other hand, the mud isn't the goal, the sawdust isn't the final product, and the muck in the stall is not the same thing as an ox. We're trying to build something glorious, and we need to be neither frightened of the dirt nor distracted into thinking the dirt is all there is.

So *be* the glory of your husband. Be the concentrated, intoxicating, incarnate poetry that tells the story of death and resurrection, and then throw yourself into the task of glorifying. Be fruitful. Build your house. Work hard. Be ambitious. Be productive. Learn more. Run harder. Take the gifts God has given you, the desires He has given you, the constraints that he has given you, and then figure out how to weave those into something glorious, something compelling, a beautiful aroma that can't be contained and that beckons a broken world to come and taste, to see that the Lord is good.

CONCLUSION:

RESTORING THE PATHS

As we look around us at our various societal ills, and there are many, the majority of our most pressing moral issues are the direct result of the women of this nation fighting for what they have declared to be their "rights." I'm not arguing that the men have had nothing do with any of this. Obviously they share a great deal of the responsibility for the smoking crater that is our nation. But there is no arguing with the fact that, while men stood around with their hands in their pockets, the *women* ran around with torches setting fire to everything and chucking on the cans of gasoline.

The most obvious example is, of course, abortion. When the Planned Parenthood sting videos came out and revealed the horrific trafficking in infant body parts that is commonplace but kept secret, our country, as a whole, was numb to it. FedEx packages filled with baby heads being shipped from one ghoulish clinic to another ghoulish laboratory—and most people didn't really seem to care. This is because for a century, we have been catechized by feminism to believe that a woman's decision to kill her baby is a basic human right, and that when a woman's body is invaded by another tiny human, that tiny human is trespassing on private property, and therefore forfeits all rights and cannot claim protection. And who has fought for that story to become the accepted narrative? The women, of course. Elizabeth Cady Stanton taught the women of her day that motherhood should be voluntary, Margaret Sanger fought for the practical rights to make that true, and Gloria Steinem has diligently worked for abortion to be seen as normal and good. For the last century, it was women who lobbied Congress, women who marched on Washington, women who published the magazines, and women who relentlessly fought for this "right." The body count is now at fifty-eight million. Fifty-eight million tiny Americans slaughtered—of the women and by the women and for the women—that the right to consequenceless sex should not perish from the earth.

One thing I found so striking about David Daleiden's sting videos (showing how Planned Parenthood makes money by selling the body parts of aborted babies) was how the *entire* abortion industry is run by women. They are not just the clients. The abortion doctors are women, the nurses are women, the CEOs are women, the people doing the under-the-table deals to buy and sell body parts . . .

all women. American mothers have outdone Stalin for body count, outstripped Hitler, run circles around Pol Pot. American mothers have waged a war on motherhood itself, and this is a war with real casualties, with real blood, and with fifty-eight million unmarked graves in our nation's landfills. And Adam called his wife's name Eve, because she was the mother of all living—and we Americans have insisted on hacking away the fertility of Eve so that the name *Eve* itself might become meaningless. "We might still be stuck with bodies that get pregnant—but at least you can't make us be the mothers of the living . . . we'll be the mothers of the dead, thank you very much."

The Hebrew word for a mother's womb is *raham*—and the root of this word means "mercy." In the Old Testament, the womb was literally the place of mercy, the woman's body the embodiment of mercy—and yet we have turned the womb into one of the most dangerous places in our nation, worse than any inner city for fatality rates, and it is the women who fought so hard for "their right" to show no mercy.

Another of our culture's obvious ailments is the utter and complete debauchery of public discourse. We are like a country that insists on running open sewage through the streets. Our pop music, popular movies, TV shows, all contain a level of filth that previous generations would not have been able even to comprehend, to say nothing of the ubiquity of porn. Now even our presidential debates are smutty. How did we get to this place? Once again, we have the women to thank. Who was it that worked tirelessly to break all the cultural taboos that had been in place for centuries? The feminists. They are the ones who insisted on talking about sex all the time, into the microphone, and refusing to ever shut up about it. They are the ones who dragged the bedroom out into the public square. One of Margaret Sanger's biggest fights throughout her life was against the anti-obscenity laws. The feminists ran a wrecking ball through public decency, and once a taboo is broken, it's broken forever. The fact that rappers can disgustingly, obscenely, gratuitously praise horrific violence against women over the airwaves and make lots of money doing it—that's a big thank you to the feminists. Earlier generations would have had those men locked up immediately.

What about our current fights about same-sex marriage? Thank you to the feminists. The feminists are the ones who fought tooth and nail to dismantle traditional marriage, and they did it *long* before the homosexuals ever started talking about it. Mary Wollstonecraft was born in 1759, remember. And in America, before the Civil War, Elizabeth Cady Stanton was choosing to remove "obey" from her marriage vows. It was the women who overthrew the ideas of traditional roles within marriage—they are the ones who tore down the walls surrounding marriage in order that they could break out. But once those walls are down, they're down. It is extremely unsurprising that other people decided to walk in.

How about all the transgender fights? Thank you, women, for paving that road. Remember, if you think about the logic of all the insistence on "reproductive rights," the thing that the women were demanding to be freed from was the constraints of their own biology. The restrictions of their bodies. They wanted freedom from *their own bodies,* which is a staggering thing to think about. And they won. But of course, once we have granted that your body can be something that "traps you in," something that must be fought against and violently restrained if necessary, we have, in principle, granted all the rhetoric of the transgender argument.

The place where we are standing right now, in a country that says Bruce Jenner is the best woman there is, a country that demands grown men must be allowed to walk into little girls' locker rooms alongside them, a country that is slaughtering the next generation by the millions, a country that thinks two men is pretty much the same thing as a man and a woman—this is what a country looks like when selfish women have won every single battle they have fought.

Proverbs 14:1 says that a wise woman builds her house but a foolish woman tears it down with her own hands. What we have witnessed over the last century is millions of women in America, in unison, tearing down their houses with their own hands—and the result is that they have dismantled this nation piece by piece. The women have been focused, tireless, relentless, and driven. They have passed the baton from one generation of activists to the next, inciting foolish and selfish women everywhere to pick up their sledgehammers and start swinging at their own walls. As we look around us, not much is left. Women are capable of great destruction, as we are now in a position to see firsthand.

But on the flip side, a wise woman is capable of *building* a house just as much as a foolish woman is capable of tearing one down. And if women can tear down a nation, women can also build a nation back up. Think of the women of Scripture who gave birth to, nursed, built up, defended, and saved the nation of Israel. Sarah, Naomi, Tamar, Ruth, Esther, Mary. These were women whose obedience had incredible results.

As we look around us, we see that American women have a lot to answer for. But there are a lot of us who would like to see things changed—so let's roll up our sleeves and start picking up this mess. The one thing to keep in mind, however, is that making a mess and cleaning up a mess are two entirely different activities, and the tools will look different. We should not look to the feminists for a business model. A wrecking ball does not look like brick-laying equipment. The feminists have been in demolition mode, and that looks like marching and shouting and demanding and lobbying. If we want to start building, it's going to look like a lot of small and seemingly insignificant acts of obedience.

We need to rebuild a nation. God has called us to take dominion over an entire planet, and we should start with the mess that is right in front of us. That's a huge job, and so we need to not be satisfied with small. If our biggest goals and dreams are to have a lot of Instagram followers, we'll have a lot to answer for on Judgment Day. But although we need to not be satisfied with small, we also need to not *despise* the small . . . because in the logic of the gospel it is the small things that turn out to be the greatest (Zech. 4:10). The two mites turn out to be the biggest gift. The glass of cold water to a child turns out to be hugely significant. So don't be satisfied with small, but don't despise the small things that are actually huge things. Learn to tell the difference. What you do in your living room with three little toddlers when no one else is there to see you actually has huge implications. (For one thing, you have three immortal souls in your charge—three people to shape who are going to live forever—how could that possibly be a small deal?) But every act of sacrifice, every act of obedience, is cementing another brick back onto the wall. Every time we joyfully take what God has given us and work to turn a profit on it—that is standing another piece back up in the midst of the wreckage. Every family that is laughing together, loving one another, woven together by a strong woman who sees the profound importance of what she's doing—that is enormously significant for the rebuilding of this nation.

In Anglo-Saxon warfare, the armies would form up in what is called a shield-wall. The warriors would stand side by side, shields in front, intertwined into a solid wall which advanced on the enemy. If a man was killed, another stepped in immediately to fill his place, because a gap in the shield-wall was deadly. If the wall broke, the enemy had a crack they could move into like a wedge, opening up the army for destruction. As long as the wall held, they could not be defeated—but you can imagine how shattering personal cowardice would be in this situation. If a man in the line turned and ran, if he broke the shield-wall from within, the whole army suffered. If there was cowardice on the *inside*, destruction from the *outside* was inevitable. Men and women have been assigned roles by our Creator, and we are woven together in a shield-wall to advance the kingdom in this world. But many women have gotten sick of their place and left the shield-wall, convinced it wasn't really important to stand there. They wandered off to find somewhere they could be better appreciated, and our culture has suffered horrible damage as a result. Women have left their places empty, and there has been no one who could step in and fill that gap, because no one, not even Bruce Jenner, can be a substitute for a woman. The wall broke, and the enemy has flooded in. Our culture is shattered, in chaos, casualties, carnage, and destruction all around us. It seems hopeless, but what if Christian women were all to try stepping back into that shield-wall again? What if we were to pick up the weapons we have been assigned and actually try using them? There are millions of us—we could make an enormous difference if we just decided to try simply being obedient.

Isaiah 58 has a beautiful promise for obedience.

> And if thou draw out thy soul to the hungry, and satisfy the afflicted soul; then shall thy light rise in obscurity, and thy darkness be as the noon day: And the Lord shall guide thee continually, and satisfy thy soul in drought, and make fat thy bones: and thou shalt be like a watered garden, and like a spring of water, whose waters fail not. And they that shall be of thee shall build the old waste places: thou shalt raise up the foundations of many generations; and thou shalt be called, The repairer of the breach, The restorer of paths to dwell in. (Isa. 58:10–12)

Let's faithfully lay ourselves down, trust in God's kindness, and truly believe that He will make us like watered gardens, like springs of water that never run dry. Let's believe Him when He says that this is how we will build the waste places—even the wasteland that is our broken country. Let's pray that it will be said of us, *These were the women who raised up the foundations of many generations, who repaired the breach, who restored the paths to dwell in.*